Budapest

NICHOLAS CLAPTON is a singer, writer, broadcaster and teacher. He has sung in opera houses and concert halls across the world and is the author of *Moreschi and the Voice of the Castrato*.

Budapest

by
Nicholas Clapton

ArmchairTraveller

First published in Great Britain in 2010 by
The Armchair Traveller at the bookHaus Ltd.
70 Cadogan Place
London SW1X 9AH

This first paperback edition published in 2017

ISBN 978 1 909961 36 4

Typeset in Garamond by MacGuru Ltd
Printed in Spain

A CIP catalogue record for this book is available from the British
Library

www.hauspublishing.com

*"And those seeking Life will make a
pilgrimage to the source of Art"*

Translated from the inscription on the fresco *The Source
of Art* by Aladár Körösfői-Kriesch (1863–1920), in the
first-floor foyer of the Music Academy, Budapest

a tanár úrnak
hálával, tisztelettel és szeretettel

Contents

Acknowledgements

To the many friends and colleagues in Hungary who have helped me in so many ways I offer grateful thanks. Some asked to remain anonymous, but of those who did not, I am particularly grateful to Mária Eckhardt, Director of the Liszt Memorial Museum, to Dr András Batta, Rector of the Budapest Music Academy, to the composer Zoltán Jeney, and to the folk musician and researcher Ferenc Sebő. In England, I am very thankful for the careful scrutiny given to historical details in this book by Robert Evans, Regius Professor of Modern History in the University of Oxford, and to my patient, diacritic-ridden editors, Robert Pritchard and Stephen Chumbley.

Foreword

Of necessity this is a personal book. There is no way that it can be a complete or definitive guide to Budapest's past, present and future musical life, nor is it intended to be. (Devotees of jazz, rock and pop should read no further: this book is not for them. To fans of the first I offer my apologies, to those of the others I do not: anyone who has felt his or her house shake to the thumping inanities of the summertime Budapest Parade will understand why.) To acquire a thorough knowledge of the rich musical heritage of Hungary and of its capital is the work of a lifetime, particularly for a non-Magyar, and my own journey is therefore still very much a work in progress.

It began on a hot summer's evening at the 1995 Dartington International Summer School, the first year when I was teaching a singing class there. Each of the tutors at Dartington normally gives a recital, and at the end of mine I was approached by a tall and stocky, distinguished-looking yet casually-dressed man aged about sixty, whose most striking features were a shock of somewhat unruly grey hair and piercingly intelligent eyes. In that most individually-accented English that I now know often characterises Magyars, he asked straight out, 'Mr Clapton, would you like to come and work in Hungary?' A moment's thought, and 'Yes' was my answer.

Thus began what I can only describe as my ongoing love-affair with Hungary, its culture and its people. No doubt, there is an element of 'the grass is always greener on the other side' in this, but from my first visit, to a very cold and snowy Budapest in January 1996 (real winter, yippee!), I was captivated by a country in which classical music is not regarded by the Establishment as elitist, and therefore despised, where students really, really want to learn (and will hardly let you stop teaching, after however many hours), and where certain old-fashioned attitudes of courtesy and overall decency are deeply engrained, both in society and in the very structure of the language. (Lest I grow too rose-tinted, Hungary needs no lessons from anywhere in the ungentle art of bureaucracy, and Hungarians can of course be as rude, pettifogging and generally difficult as any other people, but it does seem to be less of a default position for them than for some.)

I have since come to value greatly many aspects of this land-locked corner of central Europe, such as its *real* folk-traditions, its wonderful food (and drink – by no means just the world-famous *Tokaji aszu*), and its true feeling of otherness, which perhaps comes not least from the difference in the means of thought and communication inherent in the extraordinary Hungarian language. Such is my affection for what one Hungarian friend called 'not Europe, but West Asia' that, as well as visiting the country several times a year, I am engaged in a struggle with the agglutinative complexities of Magyar that will last to my dying day. To date, the radio news is still rather a battle (though the weather forecast is often easier to understand than the equivalent gabble on Radio 4). I can at last chat to old ladies at trolley-bus stops, which is a great source of pleasure to *me* – what the old ladies think they are too well-mannered to say ... To introduce my readers to some of these difficulties, I have included many original Hungarian titles of institutions and the like in my text.

On my first visit I vividly remember being ferried from the still Formica-ridden airport terminal in a seriously bone-shaking example of the once-ubiquitous 'Trabi' (that glory of Communist car-building which was basically a closed-in lawn-mower with pretensions).[1] In the decade or so since then, Americanisation of much public space has proceeded as rapidly as the outward signs of the recent Communist past have disappeared: some Hungarians deplore both equally. To Westerners many things are still ridiculously (or wonderfully) cheap, though how long that will last under the auspices of victorious capitalism and the European Union, who can say? There are things, fortunately, that no political system nor bureaucratic fiat can tax or regulate out of existence: it is one of the many small charms of Hungarian life that children, and the more courteous young men, still greet middle-aged ladies with '*kezét csókolom*' – 'I kiss your hand'!

1

Introduction with (some) history

Budapest is a beautiful city, and one of the most beautiful sights there is that to be seen from the number 4 or 6 tram as it rumbles across the Margaret Bridge in the north of the city centre. Going from flat Pest on the Eastern side of the Danube to hilly Buda on the West, a truly glorious sight unfolds before your eyes, especially on a sunny day (there are lots of those), or when all is lit up at night: turn South (downstream) and on the Pest side you will see the needle-like pinnacles of the *Országház* (Parliament) pointing skywards, while from Buda the huge Royal Palace (*Királyi palota*), *Mátyás templom* (King Matthias Church) and a hundred *műemlék* (listed buildings) peer down, with *Víziváros* (Water Town) huddled beneath. Joining them is the famous *Lánchíd* (Chain Bridge).

Real picture postcard stuff, but there is one very strange thing about it: so much of it is new, or at least comparatively so. The parliament building was finished in 1902, the palace was last rebuilt after the Second World War, the church last restored in 1896,[2] and so on. Even the Chain Bridge, the oldest permanent bridge across the Danube in Budapest, and designed by an Englishman,

1

William Tierney Clark, was only opened in 1849. Though the earliest settlement in the area dates from the Stone Age, Budapest has been so battered, despoiled, bombed, machine-gunned and generally laid waste that I sometimes think it's amazing that it's there at all. The depredations of Mongol, Turk, Nazi and Soviet have made sure that there is no equivalent to the Tower of London, Notre Dame or Cologne Cathedral: the history of the city is hidden.

Some old buildings have disappeared altogether; others remain, but only in part. A prime example of the latter is the Royal Palace itself, which now does not resemble in any visible way the first royal residence on that site, built from about 1247 to 1265, during the reign of King Béla IV. From about this time we have evidence of lively musical goings-on in Buda: in 1279 the Synod of Buda forbade congregations from listening to minstrels.[3] This *regős* tradition dated back to pre-Christian times, so one wonders at the effectiveness of these priestly strictures.

Physical remains of the palace only survive from the next century, as is revealed by a visit to the fascinating Budapest History Museum (*Budapesti Történeti Múzeum*), in building E of the present-day palace complex. There are considerable ruins here from building begun in the 1350s under King Lajos I ('the Great'); in 1361, during this reign, Buda became Hungary's capital. He was succeeded by King Zsigmond (Sigismund) of Luxemburg, who ruled over Hungary for half a century from 1387 to 1437, and during whose reign the famous Minnesänger, Oswald von Wolkenstein (1377–1445), visited Hungary several times in the king's service.[4] Zsigmond greatly enlarged the palace, and his chapel partly survives, the oldest musical monument here. It is a really hard-to-find jewel hidden in the very bowels of the History Museum and hence of the Castle Hill itself. The twists and turns of the various passages on the way to it are distinctly disorientating, especially to someone like me who has no sense of direction! It is well worth persevering, however. Not all of Zsigmond's structure, the immediate precincts of which also housed a school and musicians, survives, but after the fall of Communism the under-chapel became 'The Chapel of Every Magyar, rededicated in honour of St. István, 18 August 1990'. Extraordinarily enough, it was only rediscovered after the Second World War, having been buried for at least the fourth time.[5]

In other ways the history of the city is not hard to find at all. Hungarians, thanks to a very good education system that is only now beginning to fall apart (the depredations of the European Union may prove as destructive as those of any barbarian), know a lot about their history, and are proud of it. There are tablets and plaques all over the city to figures 'famous in Hungary' who are often virtually unknown anywhere else, musicians included. In Budapest, what's more, there are museums of practically everything: telephones, sewage, the fire brigade ... It is on the sometimes dirty and crumbling walls of buildings and in the occasionally still dusty and rather deserted display cases of museums that a lot of history can be found.

The Fire Brigade Museum, surprisingly, has one important exhibit for the musically inclined: a reconstruction (naturally) of the oldest known water-organ in Europe. There is another such in the museum at Aquincum, northwest of Budapest, where the remains were actually dug up – Aquincum was the capital of the Roman province of Pannonia Inferior for about two centuries. Hungary was on the very edge of the Roman Empire at its most extended, the Danube forming a natural boundary. Except for a few forts on the eastern bank, notably ones called Transaquincum (near the Margaret Island) and Contra Aquincum (near the Elizabeth Bridge, the next one south from the Chain Bridge), the Romans never really established themselves on the Pest side of the river. There they encountered the mysterious Jazyges, a nomadic tribe who from time to time caused them a lot of trouble. The organ in the Aquincum museum doesn't look very like the one the Fire Brigade Museum has, Hungarians are very fond of arguing. I've heard a replica actually being played: a rather wheezy and altogether peculiar sound.

I am certainly not enough of a museum 'wonk' to recommend visiting them to look at *one* thing, but I would recommend, to the musically-interested visitor as to anyone else, a good long session in the *Magyar Nemzeti Múzeum* (Hungarian National Museum). Here the whole history of the country is traced in room after room of beautiful exhibits. It's not interactive (thank God, I say), but it is very rewarding to anyone prepared to work a bit. Like most foreigners, I knew very little about Hungary when I first came to Budapest over a decade ago, and this place was a real eye-opener to the richness of Hungary's history and culture. The Carpathian basin, in which

Hungary sits, is basically a plain bisected by rivers and surrounded by mountains: altogether a wonderful bit of 'natural geography', and the peoples that have inhabited it over the centuries have been many and various.

So have their musically-related remains. As you wander, not too distractedly I hope, from room to room, you can spot, amongst others, a lovely Roman bas-relief of Orpheus (in the Lapidarium downstairs by the cloak-room and the loos) and Avar double-pipes in a case of shamanic artefacts (1st Floor, Room 8: the Avars were one of a succession of peoples to live in Hungary between the Romans and the Magyars. When you stand in front of the pipes, they play – a wonder of modern technology, and distinctly unnerving when in the Museum on a quiet, gloomy winter's afternoon).[6]

On the Second Floor, don't miss the intricately moulded stove-tile with a bagpipe-player on it from the time of the great Hungarian Renaissance. This period of growing economic development and cultural sophistica-tion reached its apogee during the reign of King Mat-thias (*Mátyás*) Corvinus, from 1458 to 1490. Mátyás was married to Beatrice d'Este, herself an accomplished harpist and a pupil of the great theorist Johannes Tincto-ris (c1435–1511), who dedicated his *Terminorum musicae diffinitorium* (c1473), the first music dictionary, to her. By this time, the choir of the Royal Chapel numbered about 40, boys and men, and was so good as to rival those of the Burgundian court and the Pope.[7] In October 1483, Pope Sixtus IV sent his friend and former master of the Papal Chapel Bartolommeo de Maraschi, Bishop of Città di Castello, on a diplomatic mission to the Hungarian court. In the midst of delicate negotiations, the bishop found time to comment that King Mátyás 'has a choir the better of which I have not yet seen. It resembles the one we had (at the papal court) before the devastation of the plague ... [The king] had a high mass sung in his chapel ... I had to realise with embarrassment that they have surpassed us in the things that belong to divine worship.'[8] Many foreign musicians also worked at Matthias' court, including the Flemish composer Jacques Barbireau (c1408–91), the outstanding Italian lutenist Pietro Bono (1417–97), and the once-famous singer-composer Johannes Stockem (1445–c1500), thought to have been resident there between 1481 and 1487.[9] There is also a possibility that Josquin was a visitor in the 1480s.[10] After the death of Mátyás, such high standards persisted: Willaert may have been in Buda in the late 1510s,[11] and the Silesian composer Thomas Stoltzer (c1480–1544) was, from 1522, master of the Royal Chapel to King Lajos II, who lost his life at the disastrous Battle of Mohács (1526), the beginning of more than 150 years of Ottoman rule over most of Hungary.

For the musically-inclined, object-spotting in the National Museum continues to be rewarding. In the same case as the tiles is a seventeenth-century harpsichord belonging to Count István Thököly (1623–70), a nobleman from *Felvidék* (modern Slovakia), and further along, from the second half of the eighteenth century, a large and beautiful green-and-gold bookcase from the library of the Castle at Vágtapolca[12] housing a lovely collection of musical instruments. Opposite this there is a baryton[13] made for Haydn's employer, Prince Miklós Eszterházy, that shares its display case with a beautifully decorated harp, said to have belonged to Marie Antoinette. Other exhibits worth looking out for include Mozart's travelling clavichord, a wonderful Empire-style 'giraffe' piano by Pest maker Wilheim Schwab, a Broadwood grand that belonged successively to Beethoven and Liszt, and, in Room 13, medals presented to the composer Károly Goldmark (1830–1915, nowadays only remembered for a few works such as the 'Rustic Wedding' Symphony, the opera *Die Königin von Saba* and his virtuosic Violin Concerto – he wrote very good songs and chamber music), and one for Liszt on his golden jubilee as a performer in 1873. Beside these is an almost madly ornate *asztaldísz* (table centre) presented to Ferenc Erkel (1810–93, composer of the Hungarian national anthem and a major figure in Budapest's musical life for half of the nineteenth century) by the instrument makers of Pest on 16 December 1888, the 50th anniversary of his conducting debut. The last rooms have heart-felt 'farewells' to the Communist regime, including a lump of the barb-wired boundary fence that formerly separated Hungary from Austria.

Of all the cataclysms to affect Budapest, the fall of Buda to the Ottoman Turks in 1541 was perhaps the greatest, at least until the end of the Second World War, since not only was it destroyed physically, but also culturally. During this period, the Ottomans had their own music, of course, the presence of which was noticed in, for example, woodcuts of the period.[14] The century and a half of domination by a non-Western culture goes part way to explain why Budapest had, for example, no public theatres until the late eighteenth century, and no specifically dedicated opera house until the late nineteenth. The centre of all matters Hungarian moved elsewhere: Pozsony, modern-day Bratislava, became the seat of government of a country, often called 'Royal Hungary', ruled by a foreign dynasty, the Habsburgs – Holy Roman Emperors, rulers (at that time) of Austria, the Low Countries, Spain and half of Italy, and one of the most powerful regnant families in Europe. Hungarian culture as such survived best in Transylvania, nominally under Ottoman suzerainty, but internally self-governing. This was the home of probably the greatest Hungarian musician of the Renaissance, Bálint Bakfark (1507–76). An extremely skilled lutenist, his compositions and transcriptions of vocal music for that instrument are still daunting to players and listeners alike, but well worth the trouble. A member of the entourage of the *fejedelem* (ruler)[15] of Transylvania, János Zápolya (who also called himself King of Hungary), travelled widely in Europe, becoming very famous and dying in Padua in 1576. In Polish, there still exists the saying 'to turn to the lute after Bakfark', as a paradigm of great daring.

Buda again suffered heavily from bombardment on the way to being freed from Turkish rule in 1686. There weren't many people left there either, and Pest was little better off. Public musical performance first returned under the aegis of the church: the records of the Jesuits in Buda speak of a positive organ being played and some kind of instrumental group performing at a ceremony to mark the first anniversary of the return to Christian rule on 2 September 1687, and in subsequent years.[16] On Easter Day 1688, a choral Mass was performed in the *Mátyás templom* in Buda.[17]

As the eighteenth century progressed, so did musical activity. By 1719, there was an official Guild of Musicians, giving the profession a stability it had previously lacked. In 1727, the first music-school in Buda was opened, in what is now Fő utca in the *Víziváros*. The church remained the centre of public musical life, church music libraries surviving from this period indicating that the repertoire performed included music from both contemporary Italy – Albinoni, Bonporti, Caldara and Perti – and from the Habsburg capital Vienna, with works by composers like Fux and Reutter.[18] Professional musicians supplemented their income by playing in inns, and the medieval Hungarian tradition of tower musicians, attached to the city watch, also survived, its members jealously guarding their status.

This was all fairly small-scale stuff, however, not least since Pest-Buda remained a small place.[19] Even in 1799, the combined population was only a little over 50,000, though the trading city of Pest had by this date, and for the first time, outstripped the old royal seat up on the hill. Vienna, the Habsburg capital, had at this date well over a quarter of a million inhabitants, London nigh on a million.[20] Pest-Buda was, however, bigger than Pozsony, and a definite change in the relative fortunes of the two cities came in 1783. In that year the Emperor Joseph II decided to remove to Buda the *Helytartótanács*

(Lieutenancy Council) of Hungary, responsible for the administration of the country and presided over by the Palatine (see pp 15–16). At the same time the Hungarian Treasury and the Military High Command was transferred, all three bodies taking over buildings vacated by recently suppressed religious orders. This resulted in a major removal of the nobility.

During this period at last, public secular performance in Pest-Buda began to acquire permanent homes. In 1776, the first public theatre opened in Pest, followed by one in Buda in 1783. The Castle District (*Vár*) remained theatreless until 1787. All of these theatres were German-language, but the *Várszínház* (Castle Theatre – now the oldest surviving theatre in Budapest) also staged Hungarian-language performances from 1790. In 1793 there was a significant coincidence: Pest audiences heard both Mozart's *Die Zauberflöte* (in German), and the first Hungarian singspiel, *Pikkó hertzeg és Jutka Perzsi* ('Prince Pikko and Judy the Persian') by József Chudy (1753–1813). For the premiere of the latter, on 6 May, Chudy 'borrowed' an aria from his great contemporary's *Die Entführung aus dem Serail*, but also acknowledged more local influences, describing two other arias as *magyar nóta* (see p 44ff). The press was enthusiastic, *Magyar Hírmondó* on 24 May commenting: 'the simplicity of the melodies touch the heart as the harmonies tickle the ear'.[21]

In the wider world this was a time of ferment, and Hungary was hardly unaffected by the French Revolution.[22] Nonetheless, on the surface at least, the Habsburg *ancien régime* carried on as normal. In any case, as far as musicians were concerned, Budapest was about to become very fortunate in its new Vice-Regent, the Palatine Archduke Joseph (1776–1847).[23] The castle of Buda had been the Palatine's official residence since 1791 and Joseph succeeded his brother Alexander to the title in 1795.[24] On 30 October 1799 he married the sixteen-year-old Grand Duchess Alexandra Pavlovna, eldest daughter of Paul I, Tsar of Russia.[25] The Palatine's next birthday, 9 March 1800, was celebrated with a concert, and rather a special one: Franz Joseph Haydn, for long in the service of the Hungarian Eszterházy family in their castles of Eisenstadt (now in Austria, then called Kismarton and in Hungary) and Eszterháza (nowadays called Fertőd, and always in Western Hungary), and by this date the most famous composer alive, came to Buda to conduct his oratorio *The Creation* (in German), less than a year after its Vienna premiere.[26] The Palatine's actual birthday being a Sunday that year, the performance took place the day before in the Great Hall (*Díszterem*) of the Royal Palace.

As if this weren't enough, the Palatine himself wished to honour his wife by proclaiming a week of festivities at the beginning of May. 'On the 7th ... a concert was held in the Buda Teatrum in which a famous musician by the name of Beethoven drew the attention of everyone to himself by his true mastery of the Forte-Piano.'[27] In this so coolly reported event he was accompanying the also famous Bohemian horn-player Giovanni Punto (1746–1803, real name Jan Václav Stich; Stich [German] = stitch = [in Italian] *punto*). The programme included Beethoven's Horn Sonata, Op 17, written for Punto, and of which they had given the premiere in Vienna on 18 April. The event is commemorated by a rather grand memorial plaque for the composer on the facade of the building, but Punto doesn't get anything, which seems a bit unfair.[28]

While having a look at that plaque, it's well worth having a look at another building in the nearby palace complex: the National Széchényi Library[29] (*Országos Széchényi Könyvtár*), which is in Building F. For a fee, anyone over the age of eighteen may use this priceless resource (if you're over 70 it's free), while there are permanent and temporary exhibitions to interest the more transient visitor. The music collection (on the 6th floor, one level up from the street) contains some amazing things. Haydn bequeathed his archive of manuscripts and other musically-related materials to the Eszterházy family, and now it is here, all 4,505 bits of it, including Gottfried van Swieten's original autograph libretto of *Die Schöpfung*. The library has acquired manuscripts by Mozart, Beethoven, Schumann and Liszt at auction, and also holds important collections of works and documents by Goldmark, and another sadly neglected, one-work Hungarian composer, Ernő Dohnányi (1877–1960), whose 'Variations on a Nursery Song' ('Twinkle, twinkle, little star' to you and me) must have become the bane of his life. Here you can also find both the autograph of Ferenc Kölcsey's *Hymnus* (1824), and Erkel's setting of it to music as the Hungarian National Anthem.[30]

Haydn only came to Budapest once, but Beethoven had later associations with another important Budapest theatre, the *Királyi Városi Színház* (Royal City Theatre) in Pest, a German-language venue, which commissioned the poet August von Kotzebue and Beethoven to write music and words for a Hungarian-themed trilogy as its inaugural production. The title of the score translates as 'King Stephen, Hungary's first Benefactor, a Prologue in one act by Kotzebue, Music by Ludwig van Beethoven, written for the Opening of the New Theatre in Pesth, February 9, 1812.' (Yes, it's *that* King Stephen, King Saint István, the first Christian King of Hungary, crowned on Christmas Day 1000.)[31] For the same occasion they wrote 'The Ruins of Athens', in one scene of which the goddess Minerva, despairing at the destruction of both Rome and Athens by barbarians, expresses a desire to see Pest, where a new home for the Muses has just opened. She descends, makes a speech in honour of the Palatine, and places a garland around a bust of the Emperor. I wonder what Beethoven, never a great 'imperialist' (his attitude to Napoleon is well-known), really thought of all that!

As in virtually every other human sphere of activity, the musical life of Budapest literally exploded during the nineteenth century. As the city's population grew from about 60,000 in 1820 to more than half a million in 1891, so this century saw the building of the *Pesti Vigadó* – a large concert hall, begun in 1816, though later remodelled (the Hungarian verb *vigadni* literally means 'to have a good time'). Here Liszt conducted the premiere of his (wonderful) oratorio 'St Elizabeth' on 15 August 1865 (later famous visitors also included Saint-Saëns and Debussy). In 1840, the Hungarian Theatre of Pest (opened in 1837) was renamed the National Theatre (*Nemzeti Színház*), and here several of Erkel's operas were premiered. As elsewhere opera was hugely popular, both the national variety and the wider European repertoire of Rossini, Donizetti, Weber and the like. For some this was too much: 'Just opera and nothing but! At the National and not at the National, and flattery and praiseful prattling in the newspapers ... we denounce these flatteries as so much vacuity, the like of which no page of history has yet produced', thundered an anonymous critic in the *Pesti Hírlap*.[32] This was before Budapest even had an opera house proper, something that didn't happen until 1884.

Parallel to this, there was a growth of institutions, both performing and pedagogic. The first professional string quartet based in Budapest, the Táborszky, worked there between 1827 and 1839. In 1835, under the auspices of the *Pest-budai Hangászegylet* ('Society of Musicians'), the city's first concert orchestra was set up. This association also founded the Pest Singing School in 1840, which was expanded into the *Nemzeti Zenede* (National School of Music) in 1867. This still exists as the *Bartók Béla Zeneművészeti Szakközépiskola és Gimnázium* (Béla Bartók Specialist Middle School and Gymnasium), with the rank of conservatoire. To quote its own website, it's 'the training school' for the Music Academy. The still-existing Budapest Philharmonic Orchestra, founded in 1853, had Erkel as its first Director, and has had only seven 'chairman-conductors' since. As well as premiering Mahler's First Symphony in 1889,[33] and many, many works by the greats of Hungarian music, its guest conductors have included towering figures from Nikisch and Klemperer to Dvořák and Stravinsky.

The establishment of these latter institutions, and such others as the Opera House, brought Budapest finally into the upper echelons of international centres of music, where it still very much thrives today. As a visitor to the city you are following such greats as Berlioz, who premiered his famously *hongroise* 'Rákóczy March' at the National Theatre on 15 February 1846; Clara Schumann, who gave recitals in Budapest in 1858, 1866 and 1868; Brahms, who played the premiere of his own Second Piano Concerto at the *Vigadó* on 9 November 1881; and Wagner, who on 10 March 1875 conducted extracts from the Ring in the second half of a concert (again in the *Vigadó*), the first half of which had Liszt conducting the first performance of his cantata 'The Bells of Strasburg Cathedral' (a real rarity), and playing Beethoven's 'Emperor' Concerto, conducted by János Richter (yes, and *that* was Hans Richter, as he's usually known – there are so many others the Hungarian element of whose origins has been obscured by changes of name or a lack of a distinctively Magyar one in the first place: József Joachim, Lipót (Leopold) Auer, Artur Nikisch, Lajos (Louis) Kentner, Jenő (Eugene) Ormándy, Zsigmond Romberg, Annie Fischer, Frigyes (Fritz) Reiner, György Széll, (Ibolyka) Astrid (Mária) Várnay and so on – and on).[34]

Musical life has certainly had its own share of bombardment and battering since the extraordinary years of Budapest's huge expansion, as in the disputes over the value of Hungarian folk music as a creative source, and the Communist regime's demands for 'Socialist realism' in music as in everything else. Suffice it to say that music has survived (of course) and indeed thrives in the Hungarian capital. Many people can still sing a folk song (or lots of them), there are still specialist music nursery-schools, and when you tell someone 'I am a musician', they don't think you mean in a rock band, and you are treated as someone just a bit special: that is a privilege and a joy.

2

Music and lightning

When I was in the early stages of planning this book, I received a rather worried-sounding phone call from a friend, the burden of which was 'you won't forget the gipsy music, will you?'[35] At the time, I remember thinking, slightly crossly, 'No, of course not, I'm not stupid', but then, remembering many CDs observed in many music shops, I wondered what the music played by the rather overdressed, perpetually smiling (at least on the record sleeves) gipsy bands might really be like. It was perhaps odd that in a decade of coming to Budapest, I had never consciously heard one. My snobby, highbrow musical instincts had always whispered that I would hate it anyway, that it wasn't serious enough, and so forth. What's more, it was only for tourists, and so couldn't possibly be 'genuine'.

The fact was that I had no real notion of what genuine meant in this case. The classical music repertoire is littered with 'Tziganes' and 'Gipsy rondos', but how far they were or are divorced from 'authentic' (oh word of devilry!) gipsy music I hadn't the faintest idea. I was started on this particular voyage of discovery by no less a person than the present Rector of the Budapest Music Academy, András Batta, with whom I had a meeting one day, and a very long talk about many matters musical. In the course of this we discovered a friend in common, a Hungarian cellist working in England, who, it transpired, was descended from a great gipsy violinist (*prímás*) of the past, Marci Banda. With the above-mentioned telephone conversation buzzing in the back of my head I asked András, 'Is there anywhere in Budapest today where I can still hear that sort of playing?' 'Oh, you must go to the *Margit Kert Étterem* [restaurant] and listen to Lajos Boross. He is the last *prímás*,' he replied, with typical Hungarian directness. Batta is a serious musicologist: I knew he knew.

Thus admonished, I went straight from that meeting to the nearest telephone directory, and phoned the Margit Kert. Were they open that evening? 'Yes.' Does the *prímás* play tonight? 'Oh yes, he is here every night.' Should I book a table? 'No need this evening, it will be quiet.'

Well it *was* a Monday, but in July tourists are everywhere, so you never know whether any restaurant will be 'quiet' in Budapest, even on a weekday. It had also been a steaming hot day, in the way that presages a storm virtually anywhere. The rain hadn't arrived by evening, but I was cautious (and English) enough to put an umbrella in my bag to keep my notebook and camera company, and that lone diner's companion, a book: Gaskell's *Wives and Daughters*, if I remember rightly (which I ended up not opening all evening). Having looked at my Budapest map, I realised that, in the previous decade, I must have passed close by the Margit Kert many, many times without ever crossing the threshold.

The view when crossing the Danube by tram is as stunning as ever, and like so many others I cry, 'Why did England get rid of its trams?' So stupid, and so much nicer than underground cattle-trucks. This evening it's route 4/6 again, also the usual tram of choice for visitors, and hence, no doubt, one of the few routes on which the anonymous Budapest Transport Company ticket inspectors will surprise travellers by flashing their blue armband and demanding to see all tickets and passes – don't try to play the 'poor foreigner' card with them: it's pathetic and it won't work. As well as joining many personally important places, such as one of my favourite restaurants in Pest, the Music Academy and a wonderful cakeshop, these trams also cross the river over the Petőfi Bridge to the south, whence there is another fine view. On its northerly crossing, just after reaching the Buda side of the river (where I sometimes get off to go and potter around the nearby antique shops), it passes the foot of the steeply-rising Margit út (street), a hundred yards up which is this restaurant's unassuming front door.

It's just after eight o'clock, and inside quiet is hardly the word. You enter between the restaurant proper and its maybe thirty-foot square courtyard, which has a central tree, tall and spreading. The former is deserted, except for a couple of flitting waiters; outside is where the action is, but there are hardly any punters. Just me in a corner and two tables of Magyars (a good sign, no gawping foreign hordes). One table: three Hungarians, two men and a woman, quiet, smoking, talking, very restrained, maybe business-people having an informal night out; the other:

two Hungarian men, of whom one is clearly a regular – fat, in his fifties, moustache, smoking like a chimney, and so obviously drinking more than is good for him that it must be the habit of years. His guest is a newbie like me, though a Hungarian, drinking it all in, ambience and booze alike. Another good sign: proper gingham table-cloths, plastic chairs, steel cutlery: this is a place of no pre-tensions, where little has changed for decades (if it ain't broken, etc).

I order Riesling to drink (Hungarian of course, it's very good), fruit soup (yes, I know it sounds funny, but it's wonderful on a hot evening), and fish. The food is fine, the waiter bored, but that is hardly the point: it's what's happening on the other side of the courtyard that really matters, and is, in a word, astounding. There are five musicians, three youngish on violin, viola and cimbalom, a fifty-year-old on the double bass, and Boross, portly, clearly elderly, also mustachioed, his grey hair carefully combed back. He is also the only one not dressed up *as* a gipsy: no red waistcoat with gold squiggles for him, but rather a sober grey suit and tie – he looks like a just-retired Budapest bank manager, but is, I gather, near his eighti-eth birthday. Except for the bass player all are seated, and were in the middle of something when I arrived, some dreamy rhapsody about a lost love or a broken heart, no doubt (it usually is).

The playing is simply fabulous: over long-held chords on bass, viola and cimbalom, Boross improvises seem-ingly endless lark-like melismas, stroking the violin strings with the gentleness of a lover; then the music breaks into fast and scurrying mode, but never hurried – nonchalant is definitely the *modus operandi*. I know enough about violin technique, but sufficient to his bow-hold is highly unconventional. Who cares? The sound he produces is of a sweetness to make any classical violinist weep, and I find that that is just what I am doing, crying into my Riesling, and feelingly completely high. No wonder Boross got the Kossuth Prize in 2006, a national award instituted in 1948, and given to figures in Hungarian art and culture of the highest calibre: previous winners include Bartók (posthumous) and Kodály – Hungary takes such things seriously, and quite right, too.

Boross' colleagues, who *are* dressed for the part, are a wonderful gallery of human types, the viola-player especially. Him I see in profile, and he looks just like a bas-relief on a Babylonian gatepost, as he tick-tocks his bow through all of three notes. The bass-player just behind is similarly impassive with *his* three notes, but there is intensity on the face of the cymbalist next to them, his skittering hammers flying across the strings like water-boatmen on a pond, producing showers of notes in a haze of harmonic infill to the music's texture. Boross' second violinist is the most stereotypically gipsy-looking of them all, his dark, curly hair immaculately oiled. His instrument murmurs and doodles in response to that of his master above, into whose stratospheric range he never trespasses. It is all so much better than I could ever have thought possible, and still the storm has not arrived, though with the music and the air pressure the atmosphere is really something. The fat, smoking diner also joins in one of the tunes, though his words are barely audible behind his facial hair and cigarette, and I very much doubt I would understand them anyway. The man is hardly singing in any acceptable sense, but Boross smiles sweetly (I think no guest could faze him after all these years) and rhapsodises on.

Suddenly they all stop and go for a much-needed cigarette, leaving the *prímás* in the garden, nursing a small glass of beer. He looks very thoughtful, and I dare to go and speak to him, for all that he could probably do with a proper break (nothing ventured, nothing gained, I suppose …). For him, I am just another foreigner, though I can speak his language to some extent, which helps. He seems pleased by Batta's recommendation (I can hardly be the first to come by that means), happy to have his picture taken (God, he must get bored with this!), and to sell me one of his CDs (at a forty percent hike of its price in the shops). My main course arrives, brought this time by a pretty, not bored waitress, and I scuttle back to my seat. Two French tourists also arrive, guidebook in hand, and sit in another corner, looking perplexedly at their trilingual menus (in Hungarian, English and German, as usual). It seems weird to hear ghastly pop music spilling tinnily out of the restaurant's open kitchen window.

As suddenly as they left, the gipsy band reappear, and this time the second violin takes centre stage, his tone darker, 'squarer' than Boross', but with a similar, fast and small vibrato; he never plays the highest notes, even when the *prímás* is resting. Again the fat man sings along, and the group are happy to do his requests, which are many – he is really showing off to his guest.

At last, and suddenly, the rain comes. The cymbalist drops everything to cover the vulnerable wooden soundboard of his precious instrument, and then goes to another corner of the courtyard to wind down a huge, green awning that will protect us all from the elements. It's cleverly built round the trunk of the tree, in the middle, below its branches, so no water can leak through. Back to the music: now it's a song about an old lady visiting a monastery (that I can make out), and the text is highly suggestive, with most of the musicians joining in as well (at last a smile from the stony viola man). Like pub pianists, they never play a wrong note, nor are ever out of tune, and they look as though they could go on all night. The thunderstorm has really arrived, with crackling lightning and rain absolutely bucketing down, crashing on the canvas awning, but nobody cares. The French couple have got their dinner (no fruit soup for them, I bet!), but are ignoring everything, one another included. Why have a holiday if you neither talk to one another nor (apparently) listen to the music? Perhaps they were under strict instructions to 'do' gipsy music, and are wishing they hadn't bothered. I'm already at the coffee stage – strong and black with a little hot milk; and I have a *körte pálinka* (pear brandy, delicious, no excuse required, though this seems the perfect time and place for it). Outside, traffic zooms up the hill, the sound oddly altered, as it always is by rain.

The band might have the energy to go on all night, but I'm feeling distinctly weary, having woken at five to the sound of rumbling dustbins, so I'm off home. The business group and the French have gone (that was quick;

bored with dinner as well, perhaps), but Mr Fat Magyar and his friend are well down a bottle of Tokaji and look as irrepressible as the musicians. Thank God I brought the brolly: it's still pouring 'out of a tub', as the Hungarians say, as I make my way back to the tram stop. Perhaps Budapesters, especially young ones, don't believe in summer thunderstorms: I'm practically the only person with an umbrella, and we all cram under the stop's plastic shelter in varying states of dampness. At least the city's public transport system comes to our rescue, as it almost always does: two minutes' wait and here comes a tram, one of the new ones recently brought into service on this route. Bought at great expense from, I think, Germany, they officially have more room, but everyone moans about them because 'there's nowhere to sit'. They certainly run very smoothly, which is great for those who have to stand, but the old rattling ones had all the charm. Those still run on most other routes in the city, and it's well worth sampling the number 2 or 18 along the banks of the Danube, for the views, the graffiti (on all available surfaces), and for the wonderful shrieking noises the wheels make as they negotiate bends and bridges. I am lucky enough to get a seat, and in the soaking night we head back to Pest. As we re-cross the Danube I look up at the Castle Hill – force of habit. Suddenly, kapow! (just like a Marvel Comic): a huge fork of lightning rebounds off the Gellért Hill, hitting the Freedom Monument with all the oomph! Nature can muster, while sheet lightning shimmers on the horizon. Thank God for lightning conductors, and thank Boross and his colleagues for an extraordinary musical evening.

~

The next morning I listen to the CD that I'd bought. Without the atmosphere and the physical presence of the musicians, it's naturally a very different experience, though the playing is every bit as remarkable. On the disc, Boross' band includes a clarinettist, whose burbling scales add another layer of heterophonic pillowing. Perhaps the most extraordinary track is what might be seen as a sop to internationalism: Boross' take on Ellington's 'Sophisticated Lady', a wild fantasy that leaves Stephane Grappelli standing. Highly recommended.

A little later I turn on Radio Bartók, Hungary's classical music station. A famous baroque violinist is playing a Handel sonata, and sounds utterly charmless and scrappy by comparison. I wonder what Bach, Corelli or Vivaldi thought of gipsy musicians?

~

A postscript: after that wonderful evening at the Margit Kert, I returned there for dinner the following Saturday, in the company of a close Hungarian friend, herself a fine musician, who also knows good stuff when she hears it. One thing we certainly discovered: the restaurant has, naturally, got into the guide books, so only go there on a weekday, and preferably out of season. Though Mr Fat Magyar, dining alone tonight, was in his usual place, Boross hardly played, the place was heaving with tourists, including a rather raucous bunch of Scandinavians, and my companion was distinctly sniffy about the music. This, God preserve us, included 'The Blue Danube', which is about as Hungarian as bangers-and-mash, and was presumably included because tourists wouldn't know the difference (if it's Tuesday, this must be Paris, Europe, the capital of Berlin, and so forth ...). 'This won't do at all', she said. 'You must come with me to the Király Étterem and hear so-and-so.' Wondering, not for the first time, whether Hungarians ever agree about anything, I naturally said yes, but have never made it to this day: it's a very expensive place to eat, and I have been forbidden from going there by the same friend until I take her there to celebrate her sixtieth birthday, quite a few years off. (Note to self: write some more books.)

⸺

When again in Budapest during the summer of 2008 I discovered that Lajos Boross is ill, and will in all probability never return to play at the Margit Kert. I feel all the more privileged to have heard him, since, though the phrase may be hackneyed, this really does mark the end of an era. Will there be a new *prímás*, or was he truly the last? In any case, I would still urge you to go there: it is a delightful place to spend an evening. One of Boross' finest pupils now leads the band, and no doubt Mr Fat Magyar will continue to vocalise through his whiskers while drinking more Tokaji than is good for him – should such a thing be possible!

3

The 'pure source'

For many a visitor, listening to gipsy music while nursing a glass of *pálinka* might seem the most Hungarian experience one could possibly imagine. However, the music played by the Budapest gipsies isn't really Hungarian at all. Though this is a subject fraught with controversy, I shall now attempt to discuss such matters as the 'Hungarianness' of Hungarian music, its relationship to Hungarian folk music, and how gipsy music fits into the picture. Few things can be stated uncontroversially about these matters, but I think I am on fairly safe territory when I say that Hungarian folk music is an essentially rural phenomenon, originating in the countryside and village culture of Hungary, and, in part at least, extremely ancient. Since this book is about music in a city I could therefore largely excuse myself from lengthy discussions about this extraordinary heritage, and thereby escape the many attached controversies, which can be as much political as musical. There is, though, a lot of both gipsy music and folk music played and written about in Budapest, so I shall persevere.

The confusion between really Hungarian folk music and what was said to be Hungarian music seems to date back to at least the early sixteenth century, when titles such as *Hayduczki* and *Ungaresca* first appear in Western European art-music collections.[36] *Hayduczki* means 'of the *hajdú*', and the *hajduk* were Hungarian mercenary foot-soldiers, their name translated into German as Haiduck and English as heyduck/haiduk. It is perhaps not without significance that the first appearance of a *hayduczki* is in Johannes de Lublin's *Orgeltabulatur*, published in 1541, the very year of the Turkish capture of the citadel of Buda. The *Oxford English Dictionary* derives the term from the Turkish *haidud*, meaning 'robber, brigand', and the word is widespread in East European languages from Polish to Albanian, as well as Italian, with various meanings of a similar kind, though often with overtones of Robin Hood. In the Balkans, haiduks survived into the twentieth century.[37]

One recently-published and authoritative source describes them thus: 'The haiduks were a product of the nightmarish closing decades of the sixteenth century in Hungary. Evicted or defaulting peasants, escaped serfs, deserters from the border fortresses, even bankrupt nobles – the haiduks were too numerous to be called outlaws but they lived outside the pale of feudal society. They were willing to fight for whoever could pay them.' In 1603, this was one István Bocskai, under whose leadership they became involved in one of the many insurrections against Habsburg rule.[38]

Their terpsichorean antics were already well-known: 'The heyduck dance became part and parcel of the peculiar tactics of the lightly armed East-European mercenary soldiers often resorting to machinations to surprise and to harass the enemy.' This is what we gather from the report of Gabelmann, a German eye-witness, about the 1595 siege of Esztergom: 'One Heyduck and two Hungarian flag bearers jumped into the moat and danced the Heyduck dance under the heaviest firing of the Turks. One would have thought one was attending a wedding rather than being in a war.'

Contemporary sources clearly reveal how the war dance, a dance linked to occasions and rarely mentioned in medieval sources, gradually developed into a dance form encompassing the entire society of Hungary (including the serfs, the nobility, the warriors of the border forts, the ethnic groups), into a general dance style of the Carpathian Basin, the most characteristic feature of Hungary's dance culture in the eyes of Europe ... Having assumed different forms they became part of the new dance and music style of the eighteenth–nineteenth centuries referred to as *verbunk*, i.e. recruiting dances.[39]

The *ungaresca* and similar were also not specifically Hungarian in any modern sense: 'it is hardly possible to see a clear musical difference between them and the *polonica*, the gipsy dance, the chorea or the allemande'.[40] The *verbunk*, or to give it its usual Hungarian form *verbunkos*, was itself a word of German origin, derived from the verb, *werben*, here meaning 'to recruit'. It included elements from the haiduk, from traditional swineherds' dances,

certain Levantine, Balkan and Slav elements,
probably through the intermediation of the Gipsies,

and also elements of the Viennese–Italian music, coming, no doubt, from the first cultivators of the 'verbunkos', the urban musicians of German culture. A few early 'verbunkos' publications and the peculiar melodic patterns found in the instrumental music of all peoples in the Danube valley, show clearly that the new style owed its unexpected appearance to some older popular tradition. The abyss of centuries was suddenly bridged over and the bourgeoisie hurriedly and with enthusiasm took over something from the lower social strata.[41]

The reasons for this desire to embrace something at least thought to be specifically Hungarian stemmed from a national resistance to the Germanic influences which had markedly increased under Habsburg hegemony. 'The language of the "verbunkos" was full of national characteristics, that is of melodic turns accepted all over the country, and the "verbunkos" stood as a symbol for all this. Its support meant association with the Hungarian people.'[42]

It did not matter that its origins were unclear: 'the foreign elements of the early "verbunkos" were absorbed, and shaded over, at least in common knowledge.'[43] By the late eighteenth century *verbunkos* had become the idealised form of Hungarian music for the educated classes: 'the towns opened their doors to the new Hungarian music ... For the member of the provincial lesser nobility, who gladly amused himself listening to a "melody without words" (*hallgató-nóta*), and later to some czardas, it was the ideal narcotic, pliant, readily adapted to personal demands, orientally ornamented, performed as it was by Gipsy bands, in the dreamily free and capricious sparkling of extempore ornamentations and paraphrases.'[44] The most significant composers in the new style were János Lavotta (1764–1820), Antal Csermák (1774–1822), and the gipsy János Bihari (1764–1827), all of whom worked in Budapest during the early nineteenth century. These, and somewhat younger contemporaries like Márk Rózsavölgyi (c1789–1848), a more classically-trained musician, also developed the culture of *magyar nóta* (literally 'Hungarian tune'), also called *népies műdal* (folk song-like art song), a repertoire of original music composed in the *verbunkos* style, and still popular today. In their hands 'its melodic and rhythmical enrichment was such that the *verbunkos* immediately became the most important expression of the Hungarian musical Romanticism. It even assumed the role of the representative art of nineteenth-century Hungary, the role of national music.'[45]

No wonder, then, that it was seized upon by Liszt and his contemporaries. Liszt had become a cosmopolitan and essentially urban musician in early youth, leaving his German-speaking Hungarian village and rural background completely behind. In this context it is worth pointing out also the linguistic divide between town and country. Until 1844, the official language of Hungary was Latin, and many of its nobility spoke little if any Hungarian. Budapest was essentially a German-speaking city. In the country, especially amongst the peasantry, Hungarian was much more widespread.

It was thus hardly wilful ignorance on the part of urban musicians in Budapest and elsewhere that made them believe in the essential Hungarianness of the music of the gipsy bands. Liszt, like many contemporary composers, both Hungarian, like Erkel and the nowadays neglected Mihály Mosonyi (1815–70), and not, like Brahms and Dvořák, certainly turned gipsy influences to very good account in his compositions of the *Ungarische Tänze/Csárdás/Zigeuner* variety, with smouldering evocations of exotic, dark-eyed gipsy maidens, wild, orgiastic dancing and virtuoso fiddling all finding a suitably romantic, and romanticised, place. Their idea of authenticity may have been mistaken, but the music they wrote was of high quality nevertheless. In Hungary, Liszt was probably the only composer to integrate the idiom of the *verbunkos* completely into his very individual stylistic vocabulary, and incorporate it into large-scale forms; but then he was a genius.

In the context of what might make Hungarian music Hungarian (or indeed French music French, English English, and so on *ad infinitum*), it may be worth quoting the critic Lázár Horváth Petrichevich (1807–51), an associate of Liszt, who wrote thus about the first performance of Erkel's opera *Hunyadi László* on 12 April 1845: 'If Hungarian music does have a future, and if one will ever be able to speak of a Hungarian school of music ... it is largely the composer of Hunyadi László who we will thank for its foundation'.[46] To modern ears, the pervading influence on Erkel's music, alongside certain elements of local colour, is, naturally enough, his great operatic contemporary Donizetti, whose *Linda di Chamounix* and *Maria di Rohan* had been produced in Vienna in the preceding two years. Petrichevich was a very conservative figure, who strongly attacked, for example, those who were striving for Hungarian independence during this period: 'his journal began a ferocious battle against every sign of progress, and attacked especially Petőfi and the writers of his circle'.[47] It is probably little wonder that this publication did not survive the turbulence of the 1848 Hungarian War of Independence. Erkel, on the other hand, achieved immortality in the minds and hearts of Hungarians not least through composing the music for the National Anthem, a stirring melody not in the *verbunkos* style.

During Liszt's lifetime, collections were indeed published of what purported to be Hungarian folk songs, but these generally confused old and new materials. (Nonetheless, some of Liszt's pieces do contain genuine folk materials: one such is his Thirteenth Hungarian Rhapsody for piano, which contains two folk songs, one of them also later used by Kodály.) There even evolved in the villages a new repertory of songs reflecting the style of *magyar nóta*. It was left to a later generation of musicians, through painstaking research (and painstakingly making real contact with Hungarian peasants) to discover what they called the *tiszta forrás* (pure source) of Hungarian music. The best-known figures in this endeavour were Bartók and Kodály, alongside such researchers as the great ethno-musicologist Béla Vikár (1859–1945). They faced many difficulties: 'You the gentleman will stand before the Székler [peasant] ... The gentleman is something hateful for the Székler ... Not surprising. The sheriff is a gentleman, so are the inspector of [the] forest, the parish-clerk, the bailiff. The parish-clerk establishes the tax, and as a result, the bailiff puts the house under the hammer. And so on, with all the other gentlemen, they are only there to make life bitter. It will be difficult to collect data, for you are gentlemen and alien to the people.'[48]

Dismissive of popular musical taste, the researchers' attitudes also met with fierce opposition in cities like Budapest: 'the majority of the middle class bitterly refuted Bartók's new scholarly and artistic ideas. The conservatives did not want to hear of "peasant music in the narrower sense", nor could they agree with Bartók that their *magyar nóta* was merely composed urban folk song ... It was unacceptable that national music could be overtly modern and that its Hungarianness would not be overly expressed. Internalizing the language of peasant music sounded like idle talk; the public wanted to hear Hungarian tunes in Hungarian music.'[49]

What, one may well still ask, did that last sentence mean? Forty years on, and after two world wars, the situation had changed radically. The eminent musicologist Bence Szabolcsi, writing during the Communist period, saw it this way: 'Having left behind Romanticism and the European musical tendencies of the years around 1900, Bartók and Kodály early realized that they must look for their Western masters in the severe and monumental world of ancient, great European music; on Hungarian soil they found the same perfection of tradition in ancient

Hungarian folk music ... the oldest and most universal treasure of the Magyar people. They recognized the only organic basis of musical development in the culture of the people. Subsequently they created a varied and universal musical idiom from the material of this popular melodic world, and expressed its contents in various, almost in contradictory ways, but with equal intensity ... Their art was not popular art. It was more than that ... The bold plan of Romanticism to raise Hungarian music to the height of universal standards, was realized in Bartók's and Kodály's work by the very separation from Romanticism. They reached back to deeper roots to attain a higher artistic perfection.'[50]

Such writing must, of course, be taken within the context of the time of its creation, and the clear source of Hungarian folk music has undergone further diversions, changes of current, and, some might say, muddyings of the waters in the years since those first great researches. This work still continues, both in theory and in practice, and the traditions of both *magyar nóta* and true folk song survive in present-day Budapest, in places of entertainment and places of study alike.

4

Halls of dance,
halls of learning

In the city today any visitor on the tourist trail (especially on the generally ghastly Váci utca in 'downtown'
Pest), is bound to be accosted by more-or-less charming
young people touting for custom for 'Hungarian Folk
Evening' entertainments. I have never attended one of
these, being suspicious that they are probably over-priced
and about as *echt* as the flamenco evenings foisted on
tourists in Madrid (in reality, the *duende* or soul of Anda-
lusian flamenco is about as distant from the Castilian
Spanish capital as clog-dancing is from the social *Geist*
of Tunbridge Wells). However, I understand that some
of them at least are very professional, and performed
by suitably folk-costumed dancers,[51] a 'village band' (or
something that's dressed up like one) and accompanied
by lashings of goulash (though quite possible of the
yucky Viennese variety, just for the *Turisten*), paprika
(where does the stress accent go again?) and Tokaji (sweet
dessert wine with goulash? – Maybe not. Under such circumstances more *pálinka* would be much better, I feel,
perhaps the only hope of salvation!).

Any hotel can direct you towards the nearest (or
perhaps the best) of such jollities on offer, but for the

rather more adventurous, any hotel worth its salt, or its goulash, should also be able to inform its guests about a good *Táncház* in the vicinity. These Dance Halls were the physical incarnation of a post-war movement interested in continuing the rediscovery of real folk music that originated in cities during the 1960s. There were many people, particularly of the older generation then living (itself born around the turn of the century or earlier), who remembered folk music and folk dances, but, having migrated to the cities,[52] had lost touch with the roots of this tradition, and moreover, had lost the practical ability to play the said melodies. Fortunately, however, there were also young urban musicians around keen to learn these tunes, with the technical ability to play them, and with a willingness to learn the style of playing them directly from rural folk musicians. The political regime of the day was certainly not averse to encouraging social cohesion and a sense of Hungarian identity through bringing together the urban and the rural, the young and the old, poetry, music and dance.[53]

This last, while probably forming the oldest strand of this section of folk culture, is also the hardest of these three to record, and it was fortunate that the extraordinarily gifted classically-trained dancer György Martin was also on hand to learn, teach and perhaps even more importantly, film dances (originally on Super-8). The importance of Martin in the preservation of Hungarian folk dance cannot be too strongly emphasised; he founded the Professional House of Folk Dancers in 1981, shortly before his untimely death in 1983, aged only fifty-one. In

1970 Martin had become involved with the still-existing *Bartók Táncegyüttes* Dance Ensemble, which, founded in 1958, was already well-known for dance works choreographed by its founding Artistic Director Sándor Timár and his colleague István Molnár. In the 1970s Timár and Martin developed methods of teaching folk dance to 'non-peasants' and of improvising peasant dances on stage. In its present manifestation, the *Budapest Főváros Bartók Táncegyüttes* (*főváros* means 'capital') looks very professional, dancers in costume, musicians not, both on stage and sometimes on *Magyar Televízió*.[54]

How 'authentic' (here we go again!) it is to present folk art in such a manner, I leave Hungarians and others much better qualified than I am to discuss (and they do, heatedly). Such manifestations are clearly a long way from Béla Bartók patiently persuading some peasant woman well beyond her 'three score years and ten' that he really was interested in hearing a song which she had learned from her grandmother in about 1830. Singing was something she said she only did in church, but he didn't want to hear that.[55] I am also reminded of a more recent story of urban folk musicians being invited on a trip to Finland: being themselves on a field-trip in the Hungarian countryside their leader asked one of their favourite sources of old songs, another old *néni* [auntie] of eighty years and more, whether she would like to come along. Somewhat wide-eyed at the prospect of 'going abroad', she thought for a moment and then asked: 'Will there be Coca-Cola?' 'Why, yes, I suppose there will.' 'Then I'll come.'

In any case the *Bartók Táncegyüttes'* home venue is now the Budapest Cultural Centre (*Budapesti Művelődési Központ*), at Etele út 55 in the 11th district (at the southern end of Buda), which can be reached on the *Gyors* (fast) 7E-173E bus from the centre of Pest, getting off at the stop for *Kelenföld–Városközpont*.[56] You can watch or, on certain occasions, join in – be brave!

What one of the founders of Táncház, Ferenc Sebő, has called its *hőskora* (heroic period) was from about 1968 to the mid-1970s, when perhaps the most famous Dance Hall was held at the *Kassák Klub*. This latter was, and still is, situated at no. 57 Uzsoki út in the now residentially fashionable *Zugló* (14th district). Recent programmes there have included productions in Hungarian of Ionesco's *The Bald Prima Donna*, Arthur Miller's *The Crucible* and Genet's *The Maids* (my, my, how times have changed! Performances of such icons of 1960s Western culture must have had old-time Commissars revolving grimly in their graves ...), but in earlier (more innocent?) days the Klub resounded to Sebő's own band, and the feet of dozens of (mainly young) Budapesters.

The Dance Halls were also popular because many young people felt they were the one and only place free of snooping, whether official or familiar. However, they didn't only do so for a comparatively free good time – they also went to learn to dance the traditional dances, because they were interested in preserving that heritage. It would be misleading to be too sentimental about the ethnological enthusiasms of youth, but surveys taken at the time show that at least a quarter, or over seventy, of the young people attending the Kassák went once a week, and that a similar proportion attended dance classes there with the same frequency.[57] This was not just another excuse for a snog and a quick fag 'behind-the-bike-sheds'. According to Sebő there are now too many places holding *Táncház* for one to be recommended above another, but you might like to try the *Fonó Zeneház* at Sztregova utca number 3, also in the 11th district (18 or 41 tram to Etele út). Not only is there a first-rate shop, open after lunch only,[58] selling a very wide range of folk music discs (many on their own excellent record label), but they also hold regular *Táncház* evenings accompanied by the best folk-bands in town (I notice Sebő's own plays there some-times), as well as tempting you with such exotica as *The Buda tango* and *Café de Sevilla* (!). In spite of these latter offerings, this is a very Hungarian place, but again, fear not: English will be widely spoken, the bar will be cheap, and people will welcome you with open arms. They may wonder that foreigners are interested in Hungarian folk-culture, but they will be very pleased that you are.

⤸

The universally-acknowledged academic centre of Hungary is the Hungarian Academy of Sciences (*Magyar Tudományos Akadémia*), founded in 1825 and now housed in a beautiful neo-Classical building in central Pest. *Tudományos* literally means 'learned, scholarly', and so this extremely august body combines the functions of the British Academy and the Royal Society. In 1953, the Academy set up an Institute of Musicology (*MTA Zenetudományi Intézet*), at first only concerned with folk music, but now encompassing the whole research field as it concerns Hungarian music – there are special departments for the study of Bartók, liturgical music, folk music and folk dance, as well the history of Hungarian music as a whole. This also has wonderful quarters, namely one of the most beautiful houses in the beautiful Vár (Castle District of Buda), in what was the palace of the Erdődy family (now Táncsics Mihály utca no. 7). This building had an earlier claim to fame, in that this noble family had Beethoven as their guest during his visit to Budapest in 1800.

Today, this noble house provides places of work for many of the most eminent of Hungary's music researchers, who are, in my experience, a very lively and incredibly intelligent bunch: musicology is not just a boring 'ology', though it can be, like any other. The palace also contains the extraordinary Bartók Archive, an enormous resource for researchers in folk music, one of the treasures of which is the *Bartók Béla Népdalok Egyetemes Gyütemény* (Bartók General Folksong Collection). This fruit of many researchers' work over many years can now be sampled online.[59] You can view frames of Bartók's own autograph transcriptions and those of the many other collectors whose work is included, just as they were done in the field. You can read them as printed scores (with variants as appropriate), and listen to them (on sound files). There are thousands and thousands of tunes, dances and songs, both hearing and seeing any of which is a seriously time-dislocating experience. The labour involved in the collection, collating, indexing, and the more recent digitisation of this archive almost beggars belief. A truly amazing achievement by a very large number of people over, all told, a century and more.

It is particularly apposite that this great research resource is now available free of charge to anyone at the end of a computer, since the Institute might seem a little forbidding in other respects: it has massive doors, and you have to contend with a maybe slightly suspicious monoglot porter in a plate glass (or maybe perspex) cupboard affair in the Entrance Hall in order to gain admittance. The physical collections of old and fragile wax cylinders and manuscripts are only available to accredited scholars working in the field, though I was lucky enough to have a private tour of the archive many years ago and see some of the cylinders Bartók himself used in his recordings.

On my early visits to Budapest, I often stayed in the old guest room of the Institute, situated just behind the above-mentioned perspex box. I remember my first forays into cooking Hungarian food; trying to work out how to say to the porter 'there is no hot water' (this only happened once, I hasten to add: generally the water was plentiful, and scalding); listening to a radio that still seemed to be tuneable only to old-style medium wave Eastern European stations; and lying on the hardest bed in the universe gazing at long dead Hungarian musical notables, whose cracked and fading portraits loomed at me from the high walls. Though this was only a dozen years ago, it now seems a world away: every stick of furniture and each of the 'fixtures and fittings' still had an official Communist adhesive label on it, so that an inventory could be taken every year, and every week elderly cleaning ladies clad in pastel-coloured nylon overalls came to change the sheets and the scratchy towels. We had wonderful sign-language-riddled conversations and smiled a lot. To sleep in this place, stony mattresses notwithstanding, was a great privilege. How many times have *you* stayed in the same hotel as Beethoven, even give or take a couple of centuries?

This guest room is now the home of the Dohnányi Archive (*Dohnányi Ernő Archívum*), an increasingly interesting place for those interested in this contemporary of Bartók and Kodály, whose late Romantic style, insufficiently Hungarian in the eyes of some, has led to his neglect (long-standing accusations of anti-Semitism did not help his reputation either, though these are now known to be untrue). Though not a composer in the same league as Bartók, Dohnányi is due for a serious reassessment. He was also a wonderful pianist, often seen in the music shop of Rózsavölgyi és Tarsa, looking through new piano pieces, so that he could memorise them for inclusion in his next recital – which just happened to be taking place that evening!

A more public function of the building is its Museum of Musical History (*Zenetörténeti Muzeum*), now undergoing refurbishment (as indeed most of the building has been for several years), but also now partially reopened just in time to hold a beautiful exhibition commemorating the 125th anniversary of the birth of Zoltán Kodály (born 16 December 1882), a father figure of the Institute and an important source of support for many years in the 1950s and 1960s, at a time when politics loomed large over research in any field.[60] The large permanent collection of the Museum, at present so deeply under wraps that I couldn't get a peek at anything, promises rich exhibitions in the future.

Another much more recently opened centre important in the study, development and preservation of Hungarian folk music in the country's capital is the *Hagyományok Háza* (Hungarian Heritage House) in the recently restored Buda Casino on Corvin tér in the 1st district. This is the home of the Hungarian State Folk Ensemble (*Magyar Állami Népi Együttes*, every bit as prestigious and old as the *Bartók Táncegyüttes*), which stages regular shows there, and of a Folk Arts Centre that proclaims that 'Our aim is to include the traditional culture, being an authentic and valid practical knowledge, in the contemporary culture, entertainment, education and everyday life, moreover, to make our cultural heritage – especially folk dance, folk music, folk narratives and handicraft – survive as a part of our universal culture.'[61] Great idea, but why not get a native English speaker to help with the translation (an annoyingly frequent omission in Hungary!)? The building also houses the László Lajtha Folklore Documentation Centre,[62] another important archive covering all aspects of Hungarian folk culture.[63]

Coming bang up to date, another interesting development has been the establishment of a Department of Folk Music at the Music Academy (now officially the *Liszt Ferenc Zeneművészeti Egyetem* or Franz Liszt Music University – everyone still calls it the *Zeneakadémia*, which has quite enough different vowels for the non-Magyar to pronounce). This had led to reactions in the Budapest musical establishment varying from pride, through shrugged shoulders, to furious contempt: one good friend of mine, a real enthusiast for contemporary serious music,[64] dismissed the whole idea with: 'These plastic peasants have no properly measurable standards, and such study as this has no place in a music academy. The tradition is dead, and you are utterly naïve if you do not think it's a farce. And their politics stink!' I am now used to such directness from Hungarians. It's not rudeness (no, really, it isn't), but think how they talk to people they *don't* like! This extremely intelligent and cultured gentleman would rather have Musical Theatre studied and performed in conservatoires, as is now done in Britain (and virtually everywhere else, it would seem – the joys of globalisation).

All I was trying to do was to describe to him my enjoyment of the first concert by students of this new department in the Small Hall of the Music Academy a couple of days before. Nineteen young people, full of enthusiasm and talent, had delighted an audience of parents, fellow students, and a few slightly bewildered outsiders (like me) with a variety of dance-tunes, love-songs and laments from all over the Hungarian world. All the singers were young women (only because, as the department's Director told me, no men had applied), who were marvellously serene in their delivery, with posture and presentation that many a student of operatic singing might envy.

Of the instruments, I remember especially a hauntingly beautiful instrument called the *tilinkó*, an end-blown shepherd's pipe presumably related to the Japanese shakuhachi, played with utter composure by a Hungarian girl from northern Serbia (the Vojvodina, called by the Hungarians *Vajdaság*); its sound seemed to come literally from the crack of humanity's dawn, with whispering harmonics colouring the melody in a unique, rustling halo. In another sense, though, this performance was an invasion from the modern world: a girl playing a man's instrument, which would never have happened in a village. Indeed, though in this concert most of the instrumentalists were men, there were other examples of such sexual equality on the stage, including two wonderful girl fiddlers, one of whom wore trousers: they were every bit as good as the boys. Another girl played a solo on the *citera*, rather like a squared-off guitar played on a table, accompanying herself with total accuracy in a typically slow-then-fast song about love, I think. There were other wonderful instruments: the *gardon*, a kind of folk cello played in a percussive way that surely influenced Bartók's introduction of 'snap' pizzicato in his string writing; and two very different looking instruments both called *tambura*, one a big guitar-like thing, the other a tiny ukulele/lute cross played with frenetic energy by a pig-tailed young man.[65]

Like Mr Boross' band, these kids never put a foot wrong. They smiled a bit when the music was fast or when the words were particularly beautiful. They were composed, they were joyful, they performed everything from memory. I may be naïve and I may be over-egging the pudding, but I shall never forget the radiance of one girl, who had no solo to sing, but whose beautiful face showed that she was utterly enrapt in the performance, while giving everything to her audience – what more can one ask from any musician?

I was very pleased to see that the whole troupe were performing next day at the Christmas market in Vörösmarty tér, the main square in the centre of Pest, at an annual folk/handcraft/mulled-wine-and-sausages (and a *lot* more) event as good as any such market anywhere in Germany (and considerably cheaper).[66] There is a stage rigged up here, with performances ranging from a Punch-and-Judy type puppet theatre telling Hungarian folk tales to enthralled ranks of children and parents, minstrels reciting endless ballads, and first-rate folk groups from across the country. It's yet another good reason, along with the weather, the food and so many other things, for spending Christmas in Budapest. Often we get proper snow, dry, crunchy, six inches deep, while on the comestibles side there is spiced fish soup, baked carp, roast goose, and the wonderful *beigli*, a pastry Swiss roll stuffed with chestnuts, walnuts or poppy seeds – what more could you want?

If you are really bitten by the Hungarian folk music bug, and are getting withdrawal symptoms after leaving Budapest, I can heartily recommend 'Folkrádió'[67], a not-for-profit, online-only radio station broadcasting twenty-four hours a day, seven days a week, and run entirely by enthusiasts. Its first broadcast was, in true Hungarian style, on 15 March 2003, the 165th anniversary of the 1848 Revolution. The first time I 'tuned in' a woman's mourning song was being sung, one collected by Ferenc Sebő himself in about 1980 near the small Hungarian town of Elek, close to the Romanian border: how about that for a living tradition! However, their programming is not exactly structured, so it's a real mosaic, and one that seems eventually to repeat itself – you can easily hear a really old and crackly voice or shepherd's pipe from a hundred years ago next to something that sounds distinctly cleaned-up, folk-guitared and world-musicified (these latter are much scarcer, thankfully). It is the women's laments, though, that get me every time, and the haunting beauty of one has just stopped me in my tracks as I type.

⌒

The subject of this chapter is a sensitive one in Hungary. As an outsider, I hope I have trodden sufficiently carefully. In the last resort, maybe it comes down to that well-worn remark that there are only two sorts of music in the world, good and bad. Perhaps I might finish by adding a few more quotations from sources better qualified than I.

A general comment:

' ... folk music has artistic significance only when, in the hands of a formative talent, it can penetrate into and influence the higher forms of music. In the hands of lesser talents, neither folk music, nor any other musical genre may acquire significance. Thus: lack of talent will be helped neither by relying on folk music, nor by relying on anything else. The result will still be nothing.'[68] (Béla Bartók)

On folk music:

'Each folk tune is a model of high artistic perfection. I regard folk songs as masterworks in miniature, as I do Bach fugues, or Mozart sonatas within the world of the larger forms.'[69] (Bartók)

On folk music in a city:

'Hungarian song resounds as triumphantly in the mouth of a child from Pest, as in a village.'[70] (Zoltán Kodály)

On tradition:

'... a German musician will be able to find in Bach and Beethoven what we had to search for in our villages: the continuity of a national musical tradition.'[71] (Kodály)

5

Opera and operetta, inside and out

Those of you allergic to Donizetti, the peculiarities of opera productions and the froth of Habsburgian operetta may feel like giving this chapter a miss ... those of you not so troubled will, I hope, enjoy it. Of necessity, the singers will remain anonymous, which is exactly what some of them deserve!

As a singer, it is hardly surprising that I should sample the Budapest Opera House from time to time. How not, indeed; even non-musically speaking, amongst the many fine buildings on Andrássy út, it stands out as a symbol of the architectural glories of Budapest during the period known as the *Monarchia*. This lasted from the so-called 'Compromise' (*Ausgleich/kiegyezés*) of 1867, that set up the dual Austro-Hungarian Monarchy, until the outbreak of war in 1914: four decades and more of peace, and rapid social and economic development (at least for the middle classes and above: many, many problems remained for the working-classes, who often lived and worked in terrible conditions, as was the case everywhere). With a still powerful aristocracy and a cultured *bourgeoisie* to serve, no wonder a new Opera House was deemed necessary. Built between 1875 and 1882 to plans by the designer of many fine Budapest buildings of the period, public and private, Miklós Ybl (1814–91), it has old-world grandeur as well as beauty, with wonderful carriage drives for both artists and audience (those were the days!). The outside is decorated, amongst many other things, with statues of famous opera composers, and the whole magnificent edifice was officially opened with great ceremony on 27 September 1884, in the presence of the King-Emperor Franz Josef I and other members of the Royal Family.

The programme on that glittering occasion was the First Act of Erkel's *Bánk Bán* and, after an interval, the Overture to his *Hunyadi László*, followed by Act I of Wagner's *Lohengrin*. Erkel, who besides being the most important opera composer in Hungary in the mid-nineteenth century (he wrote nine operas, all on Hungarian subjects), also composed songs and piano music, directed the Music Academy and the Philharmonic Society, as well as being the Opera's first Music Director.[72] Amongst his distinguished successors perhaps the most famous were Gustav Mahler (in charge 1888–91), Artur Nikisch (1893–5), and Otto Klemperer (1947–50). Puccini visited several times: to promote *Manon Lescaut* (1894), and to personally coach the cast of *Madame Butterfly* (1906) and *La Fanciulla del West* (1912). Many Hungarian operas received their premieres there, including Bartók's *A kékszakállú herceg vára* ('Bluebeard's Castle', written in 1911, but not premiered until 1918) and Kodály's *Háry János* (1926) and *Székely Fonó* ('The Transylvanian Spinning-Room' – 1932).[73] Throughout the years of Socialism, the house maintained an international standard, welcoming guest artists from all over the world. Since the régime change of 1989, things have not always been easy, but the very recent appointment of absolutely top-notch General, Musical and Production Directors should ensure the future.

For the opera-lover, I would recommend the House Tour, when you will find out all about the lovely frescoes by famous nineteenth-century Hungarian artists such as Károly Lotz, Bertalan Székely and Mór Than,[74] the seven kilometres of gold decoration (how do they measure that?), the first hydraulic sinkable stage in Europe, and all the rest. The auditorium is certainly all any red-plush-and-gilt fancier could desire. It has excellent acoustics, 1,289 seats (so it's small, but not too small), and those seats are amazingly cheap – it's almost impossible to spend over £25, even for five hours and more of *Parsifal*. That, incidentally, was a very good, traditional production, with all the magic bits in the right places, brilliant performances from Kundry (a real help) and Amfortas, Flower Maidens who really danced about rather nicely, and fantastic conducting and playing from the orchestra, often the real stars of the place. A recent *Meistersinger von Nürnberg* was a more modern production (the Mastersingers sat on giant clear plastic bubbles a lot, looking rather uncomfortable), but otherwise similar in that the orchestra (and in this case the chorus) outshone all the soloists (except Kothner). I have seen half of a very good Ring Cycle, although it's a bit worrying when the best singing in *Rheingold* is done by Freia and Mime, and a so-so *Don Giovanni* (wonderful Don Ottavio, odd production, with poor Donna Elvira wandering about on stage for half the opera, looking even crazier than usual). Also a good *Aida* (no elephants, but otherwise all present and correct, and an excellent, tiny soprano in the title role – where all the sound came from, heaven knows, but 'Ritorna vincitor' was fantastic!), and an odd double bill of Schoenberg's *Erwartung* and Zemlinsky's *Der Zwerg* (the former may be a masterpiece, but it's a very odd one; the latter is just odd).[75]

Mercifully, the German *Konzept* style of direction doesn't seem to have infected this opera house too much, although the recent, and to my mind dreadful, *Elektra* bodes ill in this regard. For that I went, all unwittingly, to the 'twin' house, the *Erkel Színház*, a little out of the centre of town in the 8th district. Originally built in 1912–13 as the privately-owned *Népopera* (Volksoper), it was remodelled inside and out under the Communists, who also renamed it. It is now a distinctly unlovable concrete lump of a theatre, very Socialist and suitably cavernous (2,340 seats). The perhaps strange renaming by a Communist regime of a 'People's Opera' after an individual may be explained by the fact that this house has ever since been the venue for the Opera House's productions of Hungarian classics like Erkel's *Bánk Bán*.

On this occasion, though, I had turned up in the hope of a half-decent *Lohengrin*. Alas, and no doubt unlike what the King-Emperor enjoyed in 1884, this was not to be: one of Wagner's descendants was directing the production, and had decided to make this great work the subject of a post-modernist makeover. The Procrustean bed on this occasion was that the whole piece became an allegory of the Fall of the Berlin Wall in 1989, and the subsequent revolutions in Eastern Europe. To call this heavy-handed was putting it mildly, since all possible clichés were wearily dragged onto the set: back-projections, modern dress, rioting peasants (sorry, citizens), bad wigs. Most of the first act looked like a rather rowdy session of the European Parliament, should such a thing be possible. The orchestra was as good as ever, but some of the singing, especially from the male principals, was seriously dreadful: shout, shout, shout, and barely a legato phrase to be heard. The crowning glory was the entry of Lohengrin himself – no swan, of course (insufficiently politically correct, I imagine), but rather a swan logo on his ... briefcase. Unfortunately this was identical to the symbol used by Swan Hellenic Tours, so this hero of the German Middle Ages looked like nothing more than a slightly harassed travel agent. That might have amused a British observer, but in Hungary it was even worse, since the logo is also that of a well-known local brand of loo cleaner. By the end of Act One, I'd had more than enough, and walked the whole mile back into the city centre in a hell of a temper, before drowning my frustrations in a decent glass of wine. The logo was such a good wheeze, I almost think the Props Department did it on purpose. (I should add that this was my only, sadly off-putting, foray to the Erkel, now closed for major refurbishment and due to reopen in 2011. I have it on good authority that some of its productions have been much better than those at the 'main' house.)

When writing a book, it is surprising how many things happen by pure serendipity, and such was the case on a more recent visit to Budapest, when I was ferreting in museums and trawling archives for the present volume. A good friend of mine, an Englishman who has lived in the city for over twenty years and brought up a family here, whilst writing and researching on Liszt and teaching at the Music Academy, phoned me one evening and said, 'There's an open-air *Lucia di Lammermoor* on while you're here. Do you want to go?' How could one resist? Great opera, a lovely setting, everything *al fresco*, and, unlike England, no, it won't rain, and you won't need your thermals by the middle of Act Two.

First stop, of course, some food to stoke us up for quite a long haul. This time it was at *Pesti Lámpás*, quite a swanky eatery in the 5th district, the inner city *Belváros*. We were early, and sat more or less alone in what was once the courtyard of a block of flats – so many Budapest houses are built round such an *udvar*. This one had been glassed over and turned into a fairly international almost-in-the-open-air restaurant: good wine, decent, but not particularly characterful (i.e. non-Hungarian) food, attentive service, though the waitress seemed a bit surprised we spoke Hungarian – obviously this is a place for the tourists, with prices to match. There was also an exhibition of particularly hideous modern sculpture, and we escaped just before the live music began: somewhat electronicised 'world' music it was to be – no, thank you, give me Donizetti, even at his most hackneyed, every time! A very pleasant place to eat, though, before the noise arrived ...

A short Tube journey, and there we were: smack in the middle of the *Ferencváros*, the 9th district, not at all a posh part of town, and there is Bakáts Tér, itself nothing so very special, but the church in the centre is really something, an extraordinary pseudo-medieval affair, again by Miklós Ybl. Was he ever eclectic! A building further in style from his Opera House one could hardly imagine, though like the latter the inside of this church is as amazing as the outside, for all that, in this case, they don't match in the slightest (the interior is all pastel-cool and calm). It was, by the way, the venue for the first Hungarian performance of Elgar's 'The Dream of Gerontius' in 1999.

Almost the entire square has been barricaded off and about a thousand plastic raked seats put up on one side. This is a serious production: full lighting, full orchestra (the MÁV Symphony Orchestra, run by the national rail company, how very civilised), professional chorus (from the opera house in Cluj-Napoca, once the Hungarian city of Kolozsvár, now in Romania), lots of people all dressed up with somewhere to go, refreshment tents, portaloos, all you could possibly want. Our seats are right at the back by the lighting gantry – there isn't an empty place to be had. Hungarians take their culture seriously, and, no, it's not just rich people here, but all sorts and conditions of men, women, and very well-behaved children. This *Lucia* is part of the year's Ferencváros Festival, better known as 'Fe Fe' to judge from the T-shirts worn by those working backstage, which does nothing if not range wide in its appeal. Other productions this year include Ray Cooney's farce 'Out of Order' (the title in Hungarian is three times as long), and the musical 'The Man of La Mancha', as well as pop, jazz and classical concerts.

Anyway, here we go. Lights up, no cameras or mobile phones, please, action. I see from the programme that one of the few non-Hungarians in the cast has a name rather too close to an English expletive (henceforward Mr F), so perhaps I should be ready for anything. The orchestral opening promises well (a promise fulfilled, from them, throughout the evening), and it's a traditional production again. No condescending *Konzept* here, though there are crucifixes scattered about, and the trees of the presumably mobile forest are still in their garden centre green plastic tubs.

Nor would the animal rights lobby be very happy: Mr F's costume (as Lucia's brother, Lord Enrico Ashton) has two whole dead foxes for shoulder pads. He looks like an exile from *Don Carlos* and sings like some people think a Verdi baritone ought to sing: slow vibrato, vowels halfway down his throat, no-ho le-he-ga-ha-to-ho a-hat a-hall, more shouting, and so forth: all very *macho*, but in the first set piece the young tenor singing Normanno actually sings him off the stage, though nobody seems to notice, and it's Mr F who gets all the applause – at least the audience know that they need to do their job properly, and clap in all the right places. The men of the chorus are excellent, looking just like swashbuckling extras from a black-and-white Errol Flynn movie, tights included.

Exit gentlemen, enter harp stage left and two rather pretty ladies, one of them (the prettier) Lucia herself, who has a great fall of chestnut-brown hair. Both are carrying vast bunches of flowers, which they are to lay at selected crucifixes (that explains it). Lucia is straight into her first big number, *Regnava nel silenzio*, and very well she sings it too, though it's odd to hear *silenzio* as four syllables rather than three. She flings her flowers up in the air at just the right moment before launching herself into the cabaletta, which holds no terrors for her whatever – all the quick stuff bang on, and just a bit of hardness in the tone at the very top. They're all miked, by the way, and Lucia's electronics do come and go rather – a pity, because she's really worth listening to.

This being a real 'number' opera, once she's done, it's the hero Edgardo's turn, and by now it's also dark enough for the bats to start swooping about – this is Walter Scott as well as Donizetti, after all: even the smaller mammals are on cue. As a Romantic hero Edgardo is, naturally, a tenor, and enters very atmospherically through the open door of Ybl's church (my friend comments on how unusual it is for a priest to give permission for a church to be thus used for something secular). The light may be fading in a suitably Gothic manner, but the tenor himself is rather crude, chewing his words and spitting them out as though he can't wait to be rid of them. He certainly gives *Sulla tomba* everything he's got and quite a lot of what it needs, in spite of (typically) not doing high and quiet at the same time (for the technically minded, that shows his *passaggio* is a bit duff, and so is his intonation up there).

Nonetheless, by the time he gets stuck into the duet with Lucia, everyone is enjoying themselves enormously and applauding to the echo. Perhaps ropey singing is an essential part of open-air opera: this is hardly the first time I've heard such, and though I may go on about it, I'm having as good a time as everyone else. Meanwhile twenty yards behind (and below) me the world wanders by, as people walk their dogs to Donizetti, watch the telly ditto, and drink beer and gossip in the oh-so-aptly named *Orfeusz Söröző* (Bierkeller).

By Act Two, Lucia's mike has been fixed, so she sounds better than ever, in spite of sometimes falling into that odd Hungarian habit of saying Italian *qu* as 'kv': 'kvesta' and 'kvesto' she sings, and, it being opera, more than once. This is a minor quibble, since Mr F is still roaring his head off at every opportunity, lunging at high notes and, unsurprisingly, given his heavyweight technique, finding it hard to keep up if he has to sing anything fast: a typical case of a first-class voice spoiled by poor singing. In matters of bad technique, however, he is totally outclassed by the other bass, who sings the role of Raimondo Bidebent, Lucia's tutor and confidant. He is dressed most oddly as a Lutheran pastor, but with a pectoral cross: an interesting take on Scottish seventeenth-century ecclesiastical dress! His manner of singing is truly dreadful: not only does he swallow his vowels so much that *il periglio*, for example, becomes 'ehl puhrehlyuh', but also literally couldn't act his way out of a (large) paper bag. When he sings 'sercrehfehtsehyuh' (for *sacrifizio*) you really can see the back of his tongue squashing his voice box: as a singing teacher, I feel his larynx's pain!

That the high voices are carrying the day is reinforced by the arrival of Lucia's ill-fated husband-to-be, Arturo Bucklaw, another tenor, who though he likewise acts like a vaguely sentient bolster, sings beautifully. His is a small-ish voice, but it's so well used: singing to make you smile, for all that he moves like a clockwork corpse. Edgardo, of course, gets really wound up at the end of this act, and by the time he gets to *Hai tradito il cielo, e amor!* ('You've betrayed the heavens, and love!', i.e. the confrontation with Lucia) he's really yowling horribly – what a shame, just like Mr F, a great voice, but …

There follows a half-hour interval, and in the queue for a drink I fall into (German) conversation with a nice Polish woman who, herself surprised at the quality of the performance, is having a great time, and quite right too. Even the drinks are cheap – a more-than-decent glass of wine for about a pound, and everyone is smoking like chimneys: no health and safety fanaticism here, thank God!

In Act Three the rumbling pastor really surpasses himself, with 'oo' vowels that have to be heard to be believed: they certainly have nothing to do with 'oo' in Italian, or any other language for that matter. His enun-ciation of the phrase *terribile sciagura* (how apposite: it means 'terrible misfortune') is truly wondrous: 'tuhreh-behlu shuguhruh' is about as close as I can get. In short, he's little more than a walking object lesson in what can be wrong with operatic singing. No wonder so many people hate it, and those who love it need surtitles even in opera houses where performances are in the audience's native language. This man has been taught to make a big noise at the cost of everything else: communication be damned, though that, after all, is what singing is really about. I would love to have a few choice words with his teacher.

The chorus is still going great guns, ladies as well, as we move towards the opera's climactic mad scene. This is really good, presented straight, with plenty of blood and melodrama. Lucia does all the demented acting one could desire, and is completely convincing both vocally and dramatically. The orchestra's solo flute, that *alter ego* to the singer's madness, adds a nice touch by standing up and facing the stage in their crazed duet: a real partnership focussing on the character's deranged state of mind. At the very end of the scene reality makes a different sort of entrance, as a motorbike roars along the riverside main road behind the square. Just for once, this is no distraction: the motor was in the right key!

It's always tough for the tenor who has to sing the Graveyard Scene after the soprano's *tour de force*, and the entirely deserved ovation that it invariably receives (it certainly did so here). As you might have gathered, I fear for our Edgardo's survival. He begins very well, not least because he also knows how to act with his voice, but when the emotion gets going, so does the technique: go, that is. When we get to *his* big tune (*Fra poco a me ricovero*) he's flat, loud, and simply vulgar. I really start to envy the customers in the Bierkeller behind me. So much effort can be heard in his singing: he looks like a hero, acts like one, dies like one, but it shouldn't all be such hard work. His mike also comes and goes rather a lot. Perhaps I shouldn't say so, but under the circumstances this was quite a relief.

Huge applause, nevertheless, for him and for everyone else, with roars of approval for Mr F and especially Lucia (big bouquets as well). What a good evening for 2,000 forints (less than seven quid) – free programme and Hungarian libretto included. Barely a chill in the air at eleven o'clock, and I even managed to get home on the last metro, which was, incidentally, not full of drunks. I shall certainly be back next year, and one day I might even understand Whitehall farce in Hungarian![76]

⌐

From the pyrotechnics of Donizetti to the more *frou-frou* delights of Hungarian operetta is not *that* big a step, and I have long been wanting to sample this latter delicacy. The Budapest *Operett Szinház*, perhaps worried that the traditional productions and values of operetta might not suit today's audiences (I daresay similar thoughts have crossed the minds of the directors of the d'Oyly Carte in Britain) are nowadays interleaving the traditional fare with musicals, both American and *klezmer*, as well as more traditional fare from elsewhere, like Offenbach's *La vie parisienne*. Therefore it's never been easy for me to be in Budapest and coincide with quite the 'right thing'. In actual fact, when it came to booking tickets for Lehár's

A víg özvegy ('The Merry Widow'), it was clear that any management fears about falling attendances are woefully misplaced. I literally got the last two seats in the house, in the back row of the stalls.

The *Operett Színház* is in Nagymező utca, fondly called 'Budapest's Broadway' from its plethora of theatres. In contrast to the Opera House's opulent grandeur it is a strawberry and vanilla ice cream building of elegance and sparkle: cream, pink and gold inside and out, mirrors and lights everywhere. It opened in 1923 (pre-war it was an *Orfeum*, a combined theatre and restaurant with those special *chambres séparées* – the building still houses a Moulin Rouge Dance Club). It is not a large house (917 seats on two levels) and I need have had no fears about being stuck at the back downstairs: the acoustic is quite dry, which suits Lehár's *um-cha* opening very well, but everything is as clear as a bell.

When the curtain rises, a traditional ripple of applause runs around the theatre: well-deserved, because the set is really lovely. When the action starts, I rapidly realise that, in this company, Budapest possesses a real jewel. Everyone on stage acts brilliantly, moves wonderfully (great 'hoofing' from all concerned), and the singing is uniformly first-rate. No wobbling, no preening, at last no shouting, and an all-round ability to communicate with the audience that is second-to-none, even though I have to work hard to follow the Hungarian dialogue. (The surtitles reproduce the original German libretto, which rather stands everything on its head, but no matter.) Lehár's music is not great by the standards of Bach or Verdi, but virtually every number has a great tune, and I am several times moved to tears by the loveliness of it all.

The production is utterly straightforward, but uses every trick in a director's book: dry ice floods the stage for the love duet, follow spots follow the glamorous costumes on the glamorous ladies, there are Whitehall/Feydeau farce poppings-in-and-out (with faultless timing), the 'whole nine yards'. One fantastic quartet, for two pairs of would-be lovers, has one tiny lady throwing one tall man round the set, and one large lady doing the same to her much smaller partner, all singing and all smiling the while: great stuff, cartwheels included, and the audience roaring with laughter. *The Merry Widow* was also famous at the time of its 1905 Vienna premiere for references to the contemporary political situation, and the (maybe slightly doctored) libretto still produces knowing sniggers this evening, as well as belly laughs: there is a referendum due here very soon, about which many Hungarians have quite understandable doubts.

It may all be kitsch (or *giccs* as the Hungarians say), but it's fun, moving and very well done, so who cares? The friend I am with hasn't been to the operetta for twenty-five years, and is seriously regretting that omission. The tickets were very cheap (about a fiver each), the bar does nice sandwiches and the enormous Hungarian pretzels called *perec* (very tasty with a glass of wine), there are lamp-carrying caryiatidic statues at the top of the stairs, mannequins in Monárchia period dress look down from balconies, people come out humming 'Vilja'. What more could you want from this 'sweet dream'?[77] I thoroughly recommend it to any visitor, however highbrow.

As to repertoire, I would advise you to avoid the modern, foreign stuff like the plague and stick to the real thing, which itself is very varied. As well as old war horses like *The Merry Widow*, there are swathes of Hungarian operettas with *Csárdás*, *Cigány* or an aristocratic title like *Grófnő* (Countess) in the title. These all mean that you'll be sure of a good time. Other than Lehár and Imre Kálmán (1882–1953, *Der Zigeunerprimás* 1912; *Die Csárdásfürstin*, 1915; *Gräfin Mariza*, 1924), some composers to look out for include Jenő Huszka (1875–1960: *Bob Herceg* – Prince Bob, 1902 and *Lili Bárónő* – Baroness Lily, 1919); Viktor Jakobi (1883–1921: his best-remembered work is probably *Sybill* from 1914); and Albert Szirmai (1880–1967), for whose once widely-performed *Mágnás Miska* (Mike the Magnate, 1916) I tried to get tickets, but was frustrated by wily Budapesters, who must book up ages in advance. Another time I'll book online,[78] and for now will make do with the 1949 film, if I can find it. (There are lots of operettas available on DVD – some are black and white with no subtitles, but still lovely.)

I suppose I should have been a little concerned about hearing the '*Widow*' in Hungarian, rather than the 'authentic' German (here we go again!). Of course, it didn't really matter a jot: so good was the performance that I think we would have all got the point had it been in Sanskrit. Of the true value of this repertoire, Kálmán had this to say: 'I know that half a page of a score by Liszt has more in it than a whole operetta of mine ... but I also know that that half-page demands a high level of intellectual concentration always attainable by only a trifling proportion of theatre-goers ...'[79] Kálmán has his own permanent memorial in the shape of a bronze statue sitting on a bench outside the Operetta Theatre, cigar in hand, waiting for the next operetta lover desirous of being photographed in his company. Beside him there is also a permanently switched-on computer display of information about him and the theatre: only in Budapest could such a thing survive – in London, thanks to some drunken yob, it would be vandalised in five minutes!

6

Music on high

A still-living Hungarian musician once opined that 'there is no Hungarian church music'. This sounds like more Communist parroting (and was a remark made in the early 1980s, before the Wall came down), but the friend who reported it to me, himself a Catholic, was so incensed by it that he went in search of the said non-existent music, and came up with a list of over sixty Hungarian composers who had composed settings of the mass since 1700, more than a dozen of them active since the Second World War. Bartók, though born a Catholic, later declared his atheism, and then, publicly, his adherence to Unitarianism: he never wrote for the Church. Kodály wrote fine religious works, including the *Budavári Te Deum* and a *Missa Brevis* premiered on 11 February 1945, in the chaos that was Budapest in the final months of the Second World War and in, of all places, the cloakroom of the Opera House! The list includes other well-known names like Liszt and Dohnányi (whose 'Szeged' Mass is very good: the same friend described it as 'a scandalously neglected masterpiece'). But there are many unknowns, probably even to most Hungarians: Ferenc Kersch (1853–1910), who, having been a pupil of Liszt and a teacher of Bartók, was also Director of Music at the primatial basilica of Esztergom in the 1890s, and has been described to me as 'the best unknown composer in the history of Hungarian church music'; and Endre Zsasskovszky (1824–82, and what a feast of Magyar sibilants!), in charge of music at Eger Cathedral in northeast Hungary, who is totally forgotten. From an earlier period Georg Druschetsky (1745–1819), who worked for the Palatine József, was certainly no slouch, and neither was Benedek Istvánffy (1733–78), organist and succentor of Győr Cathedral (between Budapest and Vienna) from 1766 until his death, whose *Missa Sanctae Dorotheae* I have recorded – it's a seriously good piece of elaborate pre-classicism in the manner of J C Bach. I might also mention the German-born Joseph Bengraf (1745–91), *regens chori* (choir master) of the Parish Church of Pest from 1784. As my source for much of this information remarked: 'There must be three hundred unknown masses in Hungary. They can't all be bad. Fifty of them may even be good ...'

Church music in Hungary has a long and distinguished history. There is a huge, fascinating and very characteristic corpus of Gregorian chant, early polyphony, and lots of hymns and the like from both Catholic and Reformed sources. Most of this is sadly unknown outside the country. Clearly there was a real flowering in the eighteenth and nineteenth centuries, and a definite persistence during the Socialist period, alongside the officially-condemned Christian faith. Churches themselves were neglected, becoming dim, dusty refuges for believers, whom the State ignored or tried to pretend didn't exist. Ironically, the Communist system kept many schools run by religious orders open: Hungary was in such a bad state after the Second World War that the new regime realised that this was the only way to keep enough of an educational system going at all. The monastic schoolteachers had to parrot Socialist Realism and soft pedal on theology, but even the *nomenklatura* sent their children to such schools, their sons especially: the Benedictine school attached to the mother abbey of Pannonhalma in Western Hungary became a sort of Eton for the Hungarian Communist Party.

Roman Catholicism is the majority faith in the country, with a large reformed Calvinist/Lutheran minority (in today's Hungary the former greatly outnumbers the latter), while Orthodox churches, especially Serbian ones, are often found, there having been a sizable Serbian community in Hungary for centuries. (Of synagogues and their music I am unfortunately not at all qualified to speak, though there have been many famous Hungarian cantors: to a certain degree the Jewish population of Budapest did survive the war, in spite of the terrible hundred-day siege of 1945. The huge Dohány utca synagogue in the 7th district is a wonderful building with a most moving Holocaust Memorial sculpture by Imre Varga. Outside the capital, Jewish populations throughout the country were systematically decimated by the Nazis and the Fascist government that came to power in 1944.)

With both Fascism and Communism firmly in the past, churches in Hungary have seen a remarkable revival since 1989. Nowhere is this more true than in Budapest, where restoration work on the great basilica and co-cathedral of St István, very near the centre of Pest, finished only recently. From the grimy, gloomy, looming ghost of a place that it became under Communist rule, it has been transformed into a magnificent marble-lined edifice, glowing with candles and mosaics, and decorated with larger-than-life statues of the royal saints of Hungary's past, and fine paintings by the great Hungarian artists of the nineteenth century. For those used to the comparative austerity of a modern, toned-down Anglican cathedral or parish church it might seem overwhelming, even tasteless (I don't agree), but imagine a somewhat smaller version of St Paul's Cathedral, begun in 1846, glistening white on the outside with an enormous flight of steps leading up to the West Door fronted by a beautiful, new pedestrian square. Inside, more blazing whiteness plus acres of rust-red marble, more enormous Victorian religious genre paintings than a cardinal could shake his crozier at, room for thousands of people, hundreds of candles, altars every ten yards, a twenty-foot high figure of St István over the high altar ... I could go on, but I'm sure you get the (restrained) picture. Consecrated on 9 November 1905, the building was severely damaged during the Second World War; restoration began in 1983 (an early sign of Communist relaxation?), and was completed on 14 August 2003, the Vigil of the Feast of the Assumption.

There is music here all the time: at the main high mass on Sunday, a large mixed choir performs from the organ gallery, sometimes Mozart, sometimes Palestrina, sometimes Liszt; the latter's *Missa Choralis*, performed on Easter Sunday to the accompaniment of the Basilica's vast organ is quite an aural feast. This wonderful music (only occasionally performed in Britain, which is a great pity) echoes thrillingly round the church's huge interior, while down below there is a congregation of over 2,000 (including 'standing room') and the celebrant at mass is the Cardinal Archbishop of Esztergom (a man with seriously grand antecedents, the 'Prince-primates'). At the end of mass, everyone, His Excellency included, sings the Hungarian National Anthem: an intensely moving experience. Should you be in Budapest at Easter, I would highly recommend this event to believers and non-believers alike. Ditto Midnight Mass at Christmas, though for both you will need to arrive at least an hour early to be sure of a seat, and, especially in December, wear plenty of layers – all that marble can be seriously chilly!

On a much more intimate scale, there is a sung Vespers in the Basilica every Thursday at five o'clock, with a small, all-male choir of about six boys and as many men, who sing the plainsong psalms for the day in Hungarian, maybe some with *falsobordone* harmonisation, and Latin polyphonic motets, usually by Renaissance composers. I have had the privilege of singing at this office on numerous occasions, and, though it can be a little difficult to work out exactly where it is happening, it's well worth seeking out. Sometimes the priests and singers find themselves dwarfed by the high altar; sometimes they are in front of the altar on the south side of the crossing, where, in a fine canvas by the historical painter Gyula Benczúr, St István offers the crown of Hungary to the Virgin Mary. There is a poignancy in so few people singing in such a huge space, but perhaps best of all is the atmosphere when this Vespers is held in the little Chapel of the Holy Right Hand of St István, on the north side of the nave. This, the *Szent Jobb Kápolna*, does indeed contain the saint's right hand, in a beautiful reliquary, and is a very holy place for Hungary's Catholics; even the most boisterous tourists seem hushed here. It has a wonderful intimacy, and has witnessed some very fine singing: I remember especially some fantastic renderings of the peculiarly elaborate Hungarian Gregorian chants for offices during Holy Week.[80]

St István's Basilica is also, and not surprisingly, a favourite venue for large-scale choral and orchestral concerts, though, in keeping with church tradition, these are always of sacred music. I was recently present at a spectacular rendition of Verdi's *Requiem*, an interesting event in many respects. By a quirk of the calendar two important dates in the Hungarian year fall close together: 23 October marks the anniversary of the 1956 revolution, that tragic anti-Communist struggle so brutally crushed by Soviet intervention, and an event that still looms hugely in the consciousness of Hungarians today. A few days later, 1 November is the Christian feast of All Saints' Day, at which time, by long tradition, Hungarians (and other Europeans, though not the British) visit the graves of relatives and friends, decorating them with candles and flowers (especially big white chrysanthemums), sometimes travelling for hours to do so. Every cemetery in the city glows with the thousands of tiny, flickering lights, a sight at once eerie and moving, with definite pre-Christian overtones (to this observer at least). I noticed that the city transport authorities laid on extra buses at this time: how very sensible.[81] Around the twin feasts of All Saints' and All Souls', concert performances of requiems, especially those by Mozart and Verdi, have become common. What a civilised way of marking these significant dates, which should indeed be a time for recollection and remembrance. I am happy to say that the repulsive American 'trick-or-treat' Halloween nonsense hasn't yet caught on in Hungary to any great extent – may that situation long continue, though I fear it will not.

From the moment I arrived at the Basilica on that November 3rd, it was clear that this was to be a real event. To mark the time of year, the high altar was decorated with vases of the traditional pom-pom chrysanthemums, and the Hungarian flag that always hangs in the chancel had two small black streamers attached to it. The performance was billed as 'In memoriam 1956', and one of the soloists was another Kossuth prize winner. Four choirs and three orchestras had been brought together, so we were clearly in for an aural assault at the very least.

Though I was forty-five minutes early, there were already several dozen people patiently sitting in the nave, and within another quarter of an hour the place was packed. Most intriguingly, the ushers were all clad in medieval-style green cloaks lined with scarlet and embroidered with a double silver cross: members of the Order of the Knights of St Istvan, I discovered ('reactionaries' I heard someone mutter, but they certainly looked very splendid, lady knights included). Though this was late in the tourist season, the building was heaving with foreigners. I was surrounded by Italians and Spaniards, who gawped at the paintings and mosaics, flashed their tiny cameras, and, as usual, talked too loudly (some of them didn't even shut up when the music started). Though the tickets were quite expensive by Hungarian standards – 3,000 forints (about £10) – thankfully there were also many locals present, of all ages. In the reverberant acoustic, the babel of a couple of thousand voices, Hungarian and otherwise, created quite an atmosphere: as the orchestra filed in they also couldn't resist the chance of a particularly reverberant warm up, the rumbling, burbling brass especially – the tuba player had a field day with his arpeggios.

Before the performance began one of the senior Knights gave a long speech, the gist of which was that proceeds from tonight would go to a children's charity. He was followed by a lady who gave some very moving reminiscences of her childhood experiences in 1956, still clearly etched on her face: invoking the Christian ideals of Faith, Hope and Charity, she especially asked us to remember those children of her age who died during that dreadful time.

Choir and orchestra were already in their places, soloists and conductor ready and waiting, and we were off. Verdi's setting of the *Requiem* has been called his greatest opera, and with reason: its emotional power and musical invention is truly staggering, and for me never lessens, even with many repeated hearings. The extraordinarily atmospheric opening was in this performance blessed with Italian Latin ('loo-chay-at', etc.), and an excellently disciplined choir. In this latter there were very few 'fishes out of water', that frequent feature of amateur choirs, where many members think, or are told, that they have to exaggerate the pronunciation of everything to the point of caricature. There was one tenor, however, who was a prime example of what might be called demented gold-fish syndrome, and another who bobbed up and down rhythmically with every phrase: music can be a spectator sport ...

Enter the soloists, who were definitely split between glamour (the ladies – soprano in grey and black and lots of glitter, the contralto in suitably contralto black and pearls), and experience (the gentlemen in their sober evening tails). Far and away the best of the quartet was the soprano, who had absolutely everything that Verdi wanted in terms of voice: a real *spinto*, she never screamed or pushed, and did all the markings in the score, with some particularly fine decrescendos, floating high notes, a proper trill, and all the other things that sopranos ought to do (but usually don't, won't, or most often, can't). The contralto, who was very young to sing this demanding music (maybe twenty-seven or twenty-eight), had a great voice, but held everything back, especially her breath, so the voice tried to fight its way out with a little non-stop shudder, and of course no legato at all – every now and again she let her chest voice out, and it was a really scary beastie. On the other side of the conductor the tenor and bass, both fairly senior, were lucky to have an acoustic that was kind to them (hiding quite a lot of wobble from where I was sitting fifty feet away), but could clearly both sing this piece in their sleep. The bass did the whole thing from memory, and stood at a slight angle to the vertical; something about him irresistibly suggested a suppliant butler in a novel by Trollope or a senior domestic in the Veneerings' establishment in *Our Mutual Friend*.

The conductor himself, Director of Music in another of Budapest's inner city churches, was sparing of gesture, but highly effective, whipping the orchestra up into a suitable frenzy in the *Dies irae* while hardly raising his elbows. The friend I was with said the noise was louder than anything he had ever heard, and wondered whether the building might fall down again (as the dome did at 3.10 pm on 22 January 1868 – it also burnt down in 1947, while the 'lid' blew off in a storm in 1982). A lot of the racket went straight up into the huge cupola, but the texture remained remarkably clear, even in such tricky bits as the *Sanctus* fugue (where the brass almost got out of control). Other things I remember: a lovely flute solo at the end of the *Lux aeterna*, which the contralto couldn't really sing at all; again, quite a lot of 're-kvee-em', 'kvee tollees' and so forth from the soloists, whom the conductor couldn't, of course, drill about their pronunciation – that just isn't done, but one is tempted to ask 'will they ever learn?' Verdi was Italian after all.[82] Another priceless sight was that of the dressed-to-the-nines lady soloists swigging water from plastic bottles during the choruses – in the context very funny, and they managed to look almost ashamed of themselves. Meanwhile the bass drummer was the only member of the orchestra to remain tieless throughout: with all the banging he had to do this was highly advisable. One chorus bass sang everything totally deadpan, *Dies irae* included – I hope he was having a nice time; and there was an amazing final pianissimo high C from the soprano soloist, completely jaw-dropping: she wasn't even from Budapest, but, I think, from Pécs, and would seriously have graced any international stage or concert platform. For the chance to hear her alone, this was quite an evening.

Such are the kind of events that one might come across at St István's Basilica, and though this is the most obvious church for the interested musical visitor to seek out, it is by no means the only one in the city with regular music, liturgical or otherwise. There is also a lovely variety of church architecture, with many beautiful baroque or rococo interiors (try the Szent Anna Templom in Szervita tér for a real gilded riot, reliquaries and statues in all directions), as well as lots of fine neo-classicism, and some wonderful pseudo-gothickry – the Ottomans destroyed all the real stuff. A lot of the twentieth-century church architecture shows you what can be done: in Britain one has become so used to the hideousness of most modern places of worship. There are frequent organ recitals all over the place, and otherwise I would particularly recommend the following: the fantastically-decorated neo-medieval Matthias Church (*Mátyás templom*) in the Castle District has very good music at the ten o'clock

Sunday High Mass (often with full orchestra), as well as frequent concerts; at the Franciscan church (on Ferenciek tere – excellent small choir); the Inner City Parish Church (*Belvárosi templom*, Marcius 15. tér); the Jesuit Church (*Jézus Szíve templom*) on Lőrinc Pap tér in the 8th district – this is particularly worth a try at the six o'clock evening mass on the first Sunday of every month, when the very fine mixed choir 'Musica Sacra' sings. I recently heard them on the Sunday after All Souls' Day: they sang Schütz, Lloyd Webber (hmm ...), and the wonderful *Libera me* by Lajos Bárdos, which should enter the repertoire of every Anglican cathedral and college choir forthwith, while their singing of 'Abide with me', in very good English, made me weep. Or you could try the church of St Teresa (*Terézváros templom*, on Király utca, near the Music Academy), which has Mass with full orchestra on big feast days, or the lovely St Michael's Church (*Szent Mihály Belvárosi templom*) at the quieter end of Váci utca (5th district), which has that and more – it is a frequent venue for excellent concerts of sacred music. Of reformed churches, the German Lutheran Church in the Castle District (Bécsi kapu tér) and the Lutheran Church on Deák tér (Pest city centre) host regular concerts, while I would especially advise a trip to the Serbian Orthodox church not far away on Szerb utca, which, as well as being a very beautiful building (recently restored), has some of the most extraordinary liturgical singing I have ever heard, even if only by a priest and perhaps one other person – a living embodiment of an unchanging musical tradition and centuries-old culture.

No longer trammelled or suppressed by officialdom, the music of the church in Hungary is obviously, and very much, alive. There most certainly *is* Hungarian church music, and a lot of music in Hungary's churches, which the musical visitor to Budapest can enjoy to the full, whether at a concert, where tickets are normally very reasonably priced (£5 or less is usual), or in the context of a liturgy. The latter will often mean sitting through a quarter-of-an-hour-long sermon in Hungarian, as well as enjoying the music, and this can be a bit of a trial. When my Hungarian was really vestigial I always hoped for one particular priest at the Basilica to be preaching, whose gestures were so theatrical that, to quote Joseph Addison, 'a deaf man might go along with him in the sense of it'.[83] In contrast the St Teresa Church had until recently a Polish priest on its staff, whose Hungarian was so halting that he even drove the locals up the wall – at least he read his homilies from a book, which kept them short.

7

On the trail of great composers

This very title might ruffle feathers, so let me come clean right away: this chapter is about Ferenc (Franz) Liszt, Béla Bartók and Zoltán Kodály, and involves quite a lot more museum visiting.

❧

The first guidebook to Budapest I ever bought was that published by the magazine *Time Out*, and my copy is now well thumbed enough to be more or less falling apart – there's a lot of useful information between its covers. However, I am still annoyed by a remark made by the writer of the section on music, to the effect that Liszt was not a Hungarian composer, 'whatever Hungarians might tell you'. This is simplistic, to put it mildly, and to find out why, a few more remarks about Hungarian history, especially linguistic history, might be useful.

What is often called 'historic Hungary' was a much larger area than the modern country, and, until the collapse of the Austro-Hungarian Empire in 1918, at least seven languages were spoken within its borders. German was to a large extent the *lingua franca*, especially in urban areas and amongst the educated classes. Liszt was born in Doborján (now Raiding in Austria), in an area known as the Burgenland. This was east of the river Leitha/Lajta, and had therefore been officially part of Hungary since AD 996, though it was ethnically majority German.[84] Liszt's grandfather, Georg, sometimes spelled the surname in the German manner, List (as it is on Liszt's own birth certificate), sometimes with the addition of the Hungarian 'z'.[85] Liszt's father, Ádám, was an overseer on an estate of the noble Eszterházy family (the same that once employed Haydn), and quite a proficient musician, playing both piano and cello. Liszt's mother, Anna, was Austrian, and though his father brought him up to think of himself as Hungarian, he never learned the language (his father only spoke it a little, as well as some Latin, which he no doubt learned during his abortive attempt to become a Franciscan). German was 'Franz's' first language, though his schooling in that tongue was rudimentary. (The dialect of the peasants of his village, Burgenländisch, is still so extreme as to sound very odd to a Viennese, and in those more hierarchical days, because of his social position, he probably wouldn't have spoken much to villagers, if at all.)

Having left for Paris via Vienna before he was twelve, French soon became, and remained, Liszt's preferred means of expression. It is ironic that he was refused admission to the Paris Conservatoire because he wasn't French, in spite of having a letter of recommendation from Metternich, the Austrian Chancellor. Shortly after returning to Hungary for the first time in 1839 he proclaimed, 'I am Hungarian', to the assembled crowd ... in French, which seems somewhat incongruous, to say the least. He wrote letters to German-speaking friends in French, and even to his mother. French was then the international language of diplomacy and, to a large extent, of the aristocracy of all nations, a social sphere with which Liszt was himself very familiar. He became such a huge international star as a travelling virtuoso pianist that one might also reasonably regard him as 'supra-national'.

This is already becoming rather complicated, so, suffice it to say that Liszt always considered himself to be a Hungarian, wrote a symphonic poem called *Hungaria* inspired by the 1848 Hungarian uprising against Austria, and, on 7 May 1873, wrote in German to his good Hungarian friend Baron Antal Augusz (dedicatee of the Eighth Hungarian Rhapsody), 'It must surely be conceded to me that, regardless of my lamentable ignorance of the Hungarian language, I remain from birth to the grave, in heart and mind, a Magyar'.[86]

Some may cast doubts on Liszt's nationality, but some others prefer to take issue with his stature as a composer. His extraordinary corpus of compositions has always been overshadowed by his reputation as very probably the greatest pianist who ever lived, and the celebrity status and notoriety that attached to him as a performer and personality in the public gaze. His Catholicism did not endear him to many during his life (it was frequently derided as a sham), and has probably not helped him since.

Most music-lovers know at least some of Liszt's piano works, and many are aware of such experimental keyboard works as the *Bagatelle sans tonalité* of 1885, but how many know more than one or two of his songs (he wrote around seventy), any of the symphonic poems other than *Les Préludes*, or the *Faust* and *Dante* symphonies, light years from Brahms' contemporary works in the Beethovenian tradition, but remarkable on their own very individual terms? As a singer, I must also mention the wonderfully original oratorios *St Elizabeth* and *Christus*, and, least-known of all, positively acres of glorious church music, from the grandiose *Esztergom Mass* (1855), and the yearning tenor solo lines of *Psalm 13* ('Lord, how long?' from the same year, accompanied by chorus and full orchestra), to the extraordinary, austere and really striking *Via Crucis* (1878–9) for soloists, chorus and organ, which you will find performed somewhere in a church in Budapest virtually every year during Holy Week.[87] During the Communist period such religious music was, officially at least, ignored, but since 1989 these 'Cinderella' works have become increasingly well known in Hungary. The general lack of knowledge of them elsewhere is sad, not to say scandalous.

Perhaps it is because Liszt is so original, so much of a 'one off', that he is so underestimated. As a musical aesthetician he is also fascinating, with uniquely personal correlations between mood in his music and specific keys (in a far more sensible way than, say, Skriabin).[88] The bicentenary of his birth falls in 2011, and would be an admirable opportunity for some straightening of the record (in Hungary there are already big moves afoot along these lines).

Debussy put it rather well in his *Monsieur Croche Antidilettante*:

> The undeniable beauty of Liszt's work arises, I believe, from the fact that his love for music excluded every other kind of emotion. If sometimes he gets on easy terms with it and frankly takes it on his knee, this is surely no worse than the stilted manner of those who behave as if they were being introduced to it for the first time; very polite but rather dull. Liszt's genius is often disordered and feverish, but that is better than rigid perfection, even in white gloves.[89]

Liszt searched and quested all his life, musically, emotionally, spiritually, and is a wonderful exemplar for the idea that to travel is always more interesting than to arrive.[90]

Travelling was certainly something Liszt did a great deal of, and even after his career as a peripatetic virtuoso was largely over he never based himself in one place permanently. From 1861 he had lived in Rome, but also spent long periods in Weimar, and from 1869, came regularly to Budapest. Here he was at first pleasantly lodged at the house of his fellow *abbé*, Mihály Schwendtner, where, from 1870–1 he held a series of 'musical mornings' that became the stuff of legend. Schwendtner's house adjoined the Church of Our Lady, otherwise known as the Inner City Church,[91] of which he was parish priest. From 1858 Liszt himself had been a member of the Third Order of the Franciscans,[92] so attended the nearby Franciscan

Church in Ferenciek tere, in which his pew is marked by name to this day.

Staying with Schwendtner was fine in so far as it went, but if Liszt was going to be a real presence in the Hungarian capital, it was clear he needed an apartment of his own. Being a man with friends in high places this didn't take too long, and, helped by Baron Augusz, in 1871 he moved into a flat a bit upriver at 20 Nádor utca (now renumbered 23, and the home, amongst other things, of several film production companies and the Commercial Office of the Spanish Embassy). Here he lived until 1873, by which time preparations for the establishment of a Music Academy were well under way. The Ministry for Religion and Public Education (interesting combination, that) took out a six-year lease on number 4, Fish Square (now No. 1 Irányi utca) to contain both a home for the new institution and a 'three-room' residence for the composer.[93] Here, between what is now the city's 'shopping drain', otherwise known as Váci utca, and the river, the first Music Academy opened its doors on 14 October 1875, and here is a plaque to prove it, put up by the National Liszt Society in 1939 (above a clothes shop with the charming name 'Tuxi Divat'). For its founder, nothing was too good: 'As to the "Plan of classes in the department for Church music, Singing and Organ," I can now only repeat my previously expressed wish that the right and able person of good working capability may be found for conducting these classes. Neither invalids nor dabblers may officiate at No. 4, Fischplatz!'[94]

When designing the Academy's first permanent home,

a neo-Renaissance building on the corner of Andrássy út and Vörösmarty utca, the architect Adolf Láng took careful note of the design and layout of both parts of the previous building. Liszt's new flat was thus similar to his old one, but much grander. Indeed, though the Academy began working from its new premises in the autumn of 1879, until January 1881 Liszt taught from three rooms made available to him at the Royal Hungaria Hotel (near the Danube, on a site now occupied by the vile building of the Marriott Hotel).[95] The building, now number 35 Vörösmarty utca, remained the Music Academy's home until the new Academy on Liszt Square was completed in 1907, and is officially designated the Liszt Ferenc Memorial Museum and Research Centre (*Liszt Ferenc Emlékmúzeum*). It still contains teaching rooms, especially those of the Church Music Department (part of Liszt's original plan for the Academy, and of great importance to him). There is also a lovely small concert hall, a fine Library, and, on the first floor, the Liszt Museum, formed in 1986 from the rooms once belonging to his flat.

In the building's entrance hall, as well as modern handwritten notices telling you where the museum is (including, naturally, one in Japanese), there is a metal plaque from Liszt's day informing visitors that 'Franz Liszt is at home on Tuesdays, Thursdays and Saturdays between 3 and 4 pm'.

Upstairs, the middle-aged lady basilisks at the actual museum entrance are clearly relieved that I can speak Hungarian, so we get off to a very good start as I go through that necessary ritual of parquet-floored museums, putting on the felt slippers, which are rather like tie-on snowshoes, and, though cumbersome, are surprisingly forgettable. The museum is by no means 'as Liszt left it', and there is a distinct feel of reconstruction about it, perhaps enhanced by its immaculate cleanliness: the floors positively glow, and everything clearly has a place, and is in it. Fortunately the only sign of the interactive is music playing, which for a moment I think might be piped, but then realise is coming from a rehearsal in the adjoining Concert Hall. When Liszt lived here, he could walk straight from his salon onto the stage, a short journey still followed (though in reverse) by postgraduates of the Music Academy on receiving their doctorates. This charming ceremony is held in front of adoring friends and relations. I remember my own graduation there very well. On the Rector's chain of office we all swore allegiance to the ideals of the Academy and to the Hungarian Constitution – I fear I thereby officially committed treason against the British Crown, but hope that this can be allowed to pass in the interests of furthering greater European integration. After splendid presentations of decorative scrolls in Latin and Hungarian with a large wax seal (no academic robes, sigh ...) we all trooped into the museum and bowed to the wonderfully romantic portrait of Liszt by Wilhelm von Kaulbach, next to his American grand piano by Chickering, with its crazily ornate silver music stand. Then there was (another) speech and a very nice party.

Of the museum's three rooms, the one with this portrait is rather grand, the next is smaller and houses (at the time of visiting) an exhibition about Liszt and Catholic Church music in Hungary (meticulously researched and demanding of the visitor – this museum makes no concessions to the lazy), while the third is the most real in feeling, being a reconstruction of Liszt's study bedroom. As well as a writing desk with pull-out keyboard, next to the rather small bed is his *prie-dieu* with prayer book and rosary, above it a lovely sixteenth-century representation of the *Volto Santo*. On another wall is a glass-fronted bookcase with something of a catch-all collection of items, not just scores and books, but also a lock or two of the composer's hair, his hat and cane, his dinner plate with knife and fork, and (slightly bizarrely) his death mask.

One curiosity: the museum unsurprisingly has models of both of Liszt's hands, one in marble, one in bronze. They are not displayed together, and one can well see why: the left looks a good twenty percent bigger than the right. This may be because they are from widely differing periods in Liszt's life: the marble left from his youth, the bronze right from 1884 – the human frame often shrinks with age.

᠆᠆

Rather than being strictly chronological on this trail (since Bartók was born a year before Kodály), I err on the side of proximity and go next to the *Kodály Emlékház* (Memorial House = Museum), a few minutes' walk north up Andrássy út at number 1, Kodály körönd (Circus).

Here Kodály lived from 1924 until his death in 1967, and though enlarged by a wonderful research archive and a lovely small recital hall, this museum is very much the apartment as he left it. It is not part of a national institution, though that is what Kodály himself was, and still to a considerable extent is. Greatly loved for his work in recording and preserving Hungary's folk musical inheritance, and hugely valued for the very important contribution his music educational methods have made (both in Hungary and abroad), his music is also very highly regarded in his home country. Its 'Hungarianness' is perhaps in some ways equivalent to the Englishness of Vaughan Williams, and maybe his reputation as a composer has suffered similarly as a result, in my opinion quite unjustly. Such national traits are regarded positively in Hungary, rather than with the inverted snobbery of the English, but his music, with the exception of a few works like *Psalmus Hungaricus*, the *'Peacock' Variations* and the *Dances from Galanta* is not as well known internationally as it might be. Most of us know the Suite from *Háry János*, but how many have heard a note of the actual opera, or realise that 'Har[r]y' was his surname?

The house in which his ground-floor apartment stands has itself seen better days, having suffered from a typical lack of maintenance during the Communist period. There is still peeling paint and a lot of cobwebs in the courtyard. Inside, things are very different. The door is opened by a more charming hangover from earlier days, a lady 'of a certain age' who beckons me towards the cash desk, and otherwise does little but hover and turn the lights on and off. My ticket is also a leftover from pre-1989: they're still using the old ones, priced at 10 forints (when the statutory monthly wage was 3,000) and overwritten by hand – now they're 230 forints, still ridiculously cheap (about 75p, in fact).

The first room is dedicated to large display cases full of manuscript scores, one of the most fascinating of which for me is in the section with the forbidding name of *Félbehagyott hangversenydarabok* (broken off concert works), namely a sketch entitled *Angol ősz* (and, in red, 'Autumn England'). A pity he never finished it. There are also charming memorials to his ethnomusicological activities: notebooks, some full of tunes notated in *sol-fa* (meat and drink to Kodály and to many Europeans, but strange to most musicians trained in England); a multi-nibbed pen for ruling staves; and a little ink stamp for the same.

I am duly preceded into the other rooms by the hovering *néni* (in this case an 'auntie' who is by no means ancient), not least since the salon really needs the lights on even on a sunny morning, its net-curtained windows shaded by thickly-leaved trees outside. Here, in spite of cords to stop visitor trespass, everything is so well preserved that it really does feel as though Kodály has popped out for a pint (or rather half a litre) of milk, and will be back any minute. The décor is heavy, the dark green wallpaper patterned with gold fleurs-de-lis. Both rooms are crammed with cushions, carpets, jugs, rugs and furniture, often with folk designs; in a corner a Chinese silk banner is rolled up against the wall, glowing dimly (but Imperially) yellow; on a shelf in a little cupboard stands a set of wine glasses, beautifully, and, what *is* rare, accurately, engraved with music. Busts of the composer peer down from bureaux and sideboards, and a poster for the first (perhaps the only) Italian version of his utterly Hungarian opera *Székely fonó* ('The Transylvanian Spinning-Room') is proudly displayed. I wonder what La Scala made of it? The further room, Kodály's study, is a paean to books. The whole far wall is a bookcase, maybe fourteen feet wide and nearly as high. All the shelves are double banked – 3,000 volumes, maybe more. Does the light-switch lady dust them?

The only other visitors are an Australian couple, 'doing' Budapest. Not knowledgeable about Kodály, music or Hungary, but genuinely interested – we have a long talk about places to see and things to do, as the traffic rumbles by outside. After they have gone, I linger a little, and, as I am leaving, Madame Light Switch faithfully follows, saving the museum's pennies by 'turning off'. Looking back, there is real gloom, and an extraordinary atmosphere suddenly pervades the place. Tiptoeing back, I feel ghosts everywhere.

Back outside in the house courtyard I meet a man coming home from walking his dog. I address his dog first, always a good way of becoming acquainted with its owner, and the latter, Károly by name, picking up on my accent, very sweetly introduces himself in English. His is the flat opposite Kodály's, its entrance steps smothered in geraniums. We chat about whether Hungary is a cat country or a dog country, coming down decidedly in favour of the latter (there are indeed dogs everywhere in the city). His rather ancient pooch ignores us completely, rather happy just to stand still for a while, it seems. Suddenly all hell breaks loose – another resident has also returned from dog walking with her much younger, larger pup, and vocal battle is joined. The antagonism between ancient hound and vulgar upstart is clearly of long duration. Károly, embarrassed, heaves his animal past the geraniums, while his lady neighbour, apologising loudly, is physically dragged upstairs by her irascible mutt, as the whole building echoes to growls and yaps.

After all that, I need lunch. On the opposite side of Kodály körönd I notice the *Körönd Étterem*, ordinary, unfancy, with a shaded yard behind the street railings. I sit gratefully under a huge umbrella (it's very hot by now). Behind me, businessmen (one Hungarian) talk Italian, while at another, bigger table, a group of young Canadians are stuffing themselves with pizza (how very unimaginative!). The waiter brings a menu. '*Tisztelettel*', he says, 'with respect': real courtesy, not the phoney Anglo-American 'have-a-nice-day' variety. The food is good, simple, unpretentious – a glass of wine makes me sneeze (sulphites?). This is a busy corner, lots of traffic, the Circle full of statues of Hungarian heroes and enormous old trees. It must be very much as Kodály left it forty years ago, I am thinking, as a bent old man totters past, looking almost venerable enough to be the composer's younger brother. On another house on the Circus I see a depressing sign of progress: a huge hoarding announces that soon this will be 'Andrássy Palace Gardens'. Well, of course it's good that these old houses are being renovated at last, but I greatly fear that behind the preserved façade it will be all international 'mod cons' and not a lot else – and naturally far too expensive for the locals.

❧

I return to the city centre on the charming, clattering and highly efficient *Földalatti*, the original Budapest underground, and the oldest in the world after London. It's now officially metro line 1, but most people still use the old name, which literally means 'under the ground'. It's also musical in its own way, with a little jingle marking each stop, *ta-ta-ta-chong-chong-ching-chong*, G-B-D-G-F#-G-E. There is a large information placard in the carriage in the usual three languages. Part of the English version reads: 'Dogs can be transported ... A full-price pass without a photo is required for dogs' – definitely a 'dog' country.

❧

My third port of call needs another trip to itself. Béla Bartók is now universally recognised as one of the greats of modern music, but this was by no means clear early in his career, when his heroic work as a folk song collector was an important element in his search for a personal style. Himself born in a small village (Nagyszentmiklós, now Sânnicolau Mare in Romania), he wrote of his folk song collecting days: 'In the so-called cultured urban circles, the unbelievably rich treasure of folk music was entirely unknown. No one even suspected that this kind of music existed ... It lives untrammeled among the people themselves. If he allows himself to surrender to the impressions of living folk music, and if he can mirror the effect of these impressions in his works, then [the composer] has recorded a piece of life.' For him, the experience of folk music had to be first hand:

> It was of the utmost consequence to us that we had to do our collecting ourselves, and did not make the acquaintance of folk melodic material in written or printed collections. The melodies of a written or printed collection are in essence dead materials ... one absolutely cannot penetrate into the real, throbbing life of this music by means of them. In order to really feel the vitality of this music, one must, so to speak, have lived it—and this is only possible when one comes to know it through direct contact with the peasants.[96]

In 1906, Bartók and Kodály published jointly an 'Appeal to the Hungarian People', asking for support in achieving a 'scientifically precise and complete collection of folksongs' and for subscribers to support their forthcoming joint publication of 'Twenty Hungarian Folksongs' (in arrangements with piano accompaniment). The response to this was disappointing, and no further such volumes were issued. On the other hand, some musicians understood at once the significance of their work and what it might lead to. Bartók's great

Italian contemporary Ferruccio Busoni (himself a composer with a complex stylistic heritage) said, on hearing the Hungarian's Fourteen Bagatelles, Op 6, in which he recognised the radical nature of the Hungarian composer's synthesis of folk elements: '*Endlich etwas wirklich neues*' – 'at last something really new'. This didn't prevent Busoni's publisher, Breitkopf & Härtel, rejecting them on the grounds that they were 'too difficult and too modern for the public'.[97]

Bartók encountered similarly divergent reactions at home. In 1911, for example, he entered his opera *A Kékszakállú herceg vára* (Bluebeard's Castle) in a competition for a national opera being run by the Lipótváros Kaszinó. The jury, headed by the distinguished conductor István Kerner, rejected the work as unplayable. Bartók considered having it premiered abroad, and it is ironic that to this end a German version of the libretto was prepared (by Kodály's wife, Emma). Besides the composer's pride in all things Hungarian, the rhythms of the two languages are so far apart, that this seems almost inconceivable. Indeed, I have often heard it said by Hungarian musicians that the opera can only be given in its original language.[98] Though Bartók told his mother that he 'knew for sure he would never live to see the performance of *Bluebeard*', it was premiered, after some considerable revision, at the Budapest Opera House on 24 May 1918.[99]

Around the time of the composition of this, his only opera, Bartók and Kodály had attempted to found the New Hungarian Music Association (*Új Magyar Zene Egyesület*, or UMZE). This partly arose from dissatisfaction at the standard of performance of his own works, and 'had as its avowed aim the organization of an independent concert orchestra that would perform the newest and freshest musical creations in an acceptable manner'.[100] The enterprise was not a success: 'this UMZE has been such a nuisance that I would like to consign it to the depths of hell'[101] he wrote, and the last of five planned concerts did not place at all, largely due to the indifference of the public. The musical establishment seemed ill-disposed towards Bartók as well. In a newspaper interview given in 1912, Ödön Mihalovich, Director of the Music Academy, remarked: 'In my humble opinion, nothing has happened in the past decade that would be a pathbreaking, great event ... What do I expect of the future? [A] Return to beauty.'[102]

UMZE received some support from critics, but others were distinctly hostile: 'Bartók's work is a pathological phenomenon rather than art', wrote an anonymous critic in the journal *Világ*, in response to the premiere of Bartók's 'Two Portraits' on 26 February 1913 – some of the audience had hissed. His ethnomusicological work, in which he was interested not only in Hungarian music, but that of neighbouring peoples (and those of North Africa and Turkey) also drew fire. In *Budapesti Hírlap* for 27 February 1913, as well as criticising the new work for its resemblances to the music of Debussy and Strauss, Emil Haraszti wrote: 'We should like to know why Béla Bartók, a professor at the National Hungarian Royal Academy of Music has now assumed the role of a musical Scotus Viator.[103] Can it be that he is no longer interested in Hungarian music of any kind? He has become the apostle of Czech, Romanian, Slovak and God knows what other kind of music – any kind except Hungarian.'[104]

In the tense pre-war atmosphere, this was tantamount to accusing Bartók of treason, so it is little wonder that he now decided to withdraw from public life. In 1913, he wrote

> ... a year ago sentence of death was officially pronounced on me as a composer. Either those people are right, in which case I am an untalented bungler; or I am right, and it's they who are the idiots. In either event, this means that between myself and them (that is, our musical leaders; Hubay, etc.) there can be no discussion of music, still less any joint action ... I have resigned to write for my writing-desk only ... So far as appearances abroad are concerned, all my efforts during the last 8 years have proved to be in vain. I got tired of it ... My public appearances are confined to *one sole field*: I will do anything to further my research in musical folklore ...[105]

Bartók indeed devoted himself largely to ethnomusicological research during the next few years, though this itself was somewhat curtailed by the course of the First World War. Musical life in Budapest continued, however, and the public success of his ballet, *A fából faragott királyfi* ('The Wooden Prince'), premiered on 12 May 1917 was an important turning point. The end of the war was a period of great turmoil and instability,[106] but after this a more generally recognised success slowly came to him. On 19 November 1925, for example, when the Prague Philharmonic, on a tour to Budapest, played Bartók's *Dance Suite*, so positive was the audience reaction that an encore was demanded.

After the war, Bartók and his family had moved back to the centre of Budapest from the house in Rákoshegy,[107] where they had lived since 1912. The composer often had problems with noise when working, and three subsequent dwellings proved unsatisfactory in this respect. In 1932, hoping that what turned out to be his final house in Budapest would solve these difficulties, he and his family moved to number 27 Csalán utca, in the always fashionable Buda Hills. Sadly for his concentration, he found no peace, soon discovering that his new home was far too close to where training sessions for the annual Gugger Hill motorcycle race were held. In 1936, construction of new houses on either side of his also began (it was at this time that the house was renumbered 29), and Bartók resorted to earplugs and even built a little machine to hum continuously while he worked: all to no avail. In any case, peace of any kind was soon under threat, and the outbreak of war brought politics back into his life. In March 1940, having already been made 'deputy civil defence commander' for the immediately surrounding houses, he was required to complete a 'control residence' form. Such symptoms of an oppressive regime distressed him greatly, and on 20 October he left for a tour of America. Though originally intending to return the following year, he never did, and died in New York on 26 September 1945. In one of his last letters he wrote: 'Heaven knows how many years it will be before Hungary can pull herself together in some measure (if at all). And yet I, too, would like to return, for good ...'[108]

Csalán út is quite a trek, especially on a very hot day, as when I first went there, only to find everything closed for renovation. This now completed, I returned last summer, and found a very spick and span affair, perhaps too much so. Behind a white-painted gate, a winding path leads to the house, with a bronze stag from the 'Cantata Profana' on the lawn. Higher up, Imre Varga's statue of Bartók gazes serenely at the greenery.[109]

The grandeur of the house itself reflects Bartók's status as an eventually successful composer, and quite a lot has been added to make a museum out of it, including a large glass-clad staircase and another charming small concert hall. There is much less clutter than at Kodály's place, and consequently much less presence. (This is a difficult balance to achieve, and I'm sure today's 'best museum practice' would prefer the Bartók house.) In the composer's carefully arranged study stands his desk, identical to Kodály's and made by the same Transylvanian craftsman, György Gyugyi Péntek – there are none others quite like them. Another room, made to look like a drawing room, though a little too tidy, has more beautiful Transylvanian furniture, as pristine as the day it was made, and of a style that seems as old as the Carpathian mountains themselves (a hundred years on one can still buy it, old and new – at a price). The tour is guided, very informative and knowledgeable in its natter, natter, natter, the young woman's English very good, but typically accented. Like most non-native speakers, Hungarians find the idea of the diphthong, that messy English vocalic slither, quite alien, and who can blame them?

Upstairs, the attic has been arranged with more conventional display cases, from which one discovers that Bartók was an inveterate collector of many things, not just folk songs. As well as beetles and bugs, there are dried flowers and plants, shells, rocks and coral, alongside beautiful traditional clothes, ceramics and folk textiles, and such personal effects as six pairs of glasses, pairs of sandals and clogs, his own copy of 'Don Quixote' (in Tieck's German translation), cufflinks, and the butt of a cigarette found inside his Bösendorfer piano after he had gone to America (Bartók was a heavy smoker, and 'rolled his own').

Downstairs there is a little shop, very well stocked and organised, very up to date. The whole museum is a modern and international place for an internationally great modern composer. Some, unjustifiably I think, doubt Liszt's greatness as a composer. Perhaps Kodály's greatness is confined to the Hungarian consciousness. In contrast to the latter's basically late Romantic compositional idiom, Bartók's music can be 'difficult', but of his international stature as a composer there can be no doubt. Brought up in the all-embracing German Romantic style, he learned and assimilated an enormous amount from such great masters as Brahms, Beethoven and Bach, but discovered in Hungarian folk song the perfect catalyst and source of inspiration for his own compositional language, transmuting that ancient music into an idiom that produced works of a quality unsurpassed by any other composer of his time (with no apologies to Stravinsky or Schoenberg, amongst others). Of Bartók the complete musician, a Hungarian friend, one of the best musicians I know, once said, 'there are emotions looking for notes, and there are notes inspiring emotions. For a real musician the notes make the emotion. For Bartók music was the whole world.'

After this immersion in Bartók's world, more refreshment was needed, and I definitely felt a cake 'coming on'. A few minutes' walk down Pasaréti út was a marvellous *cukrászda* (cake shop cum coffee house): nothing fancy, a place for the locals, where an excellent *túrótorta* (creamy cheesecake with fruit) and a very good coffee costs the princely sum of £2 (oh frabjous day …). No wonder one's days in Budapest can so easily turn into a round of coffee and cake, lunch, coffee and cake, glass of wine, dinner, coffee, Unicum (yes, I know everyone loathes this cough-mixturish national poison of a liqueur, but I love it!), and so on the next day, and the next. No wonder, either, that the Hungarian average male life expectancy was one of the lowest in Europe a few years ago, alongside, it appears, that of Scotland (all those deep-fried Mars Bars, I suppose). I ought to watch it, and my waistline!

8

What, no singing?
(Well, almost ...)

Though being a singer is a wonderful life, it can leave me sometimes feeling a little inadequate when writing about purely instrumental performances. Many singers would say that even the best instrumentalists and conductors don't always know good singing from bad, so the reverse is probably true as well. Perhaps, indeed, the remark about 'musicians *and* singers' is not without foundation. I also find myself going to rather few concerts that do not somehow involve the human voice, which, at least in part, shows that I am a glutton for punishment. I find it very hard to turn off the pedagogic part of my singing teacher's brain, and not wince at some of the noises I hear.

It was, therefore, quite a relief to be invited to a purely orchestral concert at the Hungarian Academy of Sciences (*Magyar Tudományos Akadémia*). The exterior of this building in Roosevelt tér (close to the river in central Pest) is a rather sternly ornate bit of neo-Renaissance architecture from the 1860s, designed by Friedrich August Stüler. Inside it is gentler, with sweeping staircases leading to a succession of rooms of greater or lesser grandiosity. This concert was in the biggest and grandest, the Ceremonial Hall (*Díszterem*). Against a beautiful fresco backdrop of suitably historical scenes from Hungary's past, a small orchestra with grand piano centre stage was laid out in front of chairs for about 400 – and the place was packed. As is often the case in Budapest, and pleasantly so, the audience was of the type that likes to dress up a bit for an evening. I, unfortunately, had arrived in a tremendous rush, and managed to be both underdressed and loud (a bright orange jumper really stands out in such company, and my ticket was for a seat in the front row).

Unless with the prior agreement of those concerned, people appearing in this book have generally remained anonymous. I'm going to break this rule here, simply because this concert was so good. The performers were the *Budapesti Vonósok* with soloist Nicolas (Nico) Namoradze, a brilliant young pianist from Georgia, at school in Budapest, and studying under the auspices of the Music Academy's special Training School for Exceptionally Gifted Children (*Kivételes Tehetségű Gyermekek Képzője*). He is one of those extraordinary humans, who, as well as being top of every class and speaking four languages fluently (including perfect, barely-accented English), is a thoroughly nice, utterly intelligent teenage adult (he's good at football, too).

Though the orchestra's name means 'Budapest Strings', they also often use other instruments, and so the first item on the programme, Handel's Concerto Grosso in B-flat major, Op 3, No 2, had some very sprightly playing from oboes and bassoon, as well as lovely work from the continuo harpsichordist. Then Nico came on to play Bach's Harpsichord Concerto in A major, BWV 1055, and to

t as well. This he did with modest aplomb and
test of gestures. It was clear that the orchestra
..spected his musicianship, and I challenge any diehard
of 'historically informed performance' not to have been
taken with his playing – on a nine-foot Steinway it was
both breathtakingly accurate and poetic.

A quick rush to the bar for a glass of Hungarian cham-
pagne (*pezsgő* – the dry is good, I'm not so keen on the
sweet), and then back for Part Two. Lovely phrasing from
the orchestra in Mendelssohn's String Symphony in B
minor, and then here was Nico again, for a real *tour de
force*, Mozart's Piano Concerto in A major, K 488. This is
a test for a Mozartian of any age, and our soloist certainly
rose to the challenge, improvising his own cadenzas (new
every time, I understand) and really not putting a foot
wrong. He also had more real conducting to do, and there
was a wonderful moment in the last movement, when
the very fast speed he set challenged the orchestra's first
bassoon to play a solo with some of the fastest semiquavers known to man. Honour was saved, if only just, but
then they had to do the whole last movement again, such
was the applause. This included the inevitable *vastaps*
('iron clapping'), when most of the audience applauds to
a regular beat. To some ears it might sound a little too
like the umpteenth congress of The Party, but in Hungary
it really means, 'We want more!' And they got it, even
a little faster still – how the bassoonist wasn't bleeding
from the tongue (and maybe the ears?) by the end, heaven
knows, but all went swimmingly, and all went home satis-
fied. In this, the first of a concert series fittingly entitled

'Meeting of Generations', the high reputation of Hungarian orchestral playing had been triumphantly confirmed, and I had heard a *very* talented young pianist.

Though it is an extraordinarily distinguished place, the Academy of Sciences is not perhaps the natural home of Budapest's concert giving, which for very many years has been the Great Hall of the Music Academy, on Liszt tér. This must surely be one of the world's loveliest concert halls, its supremely elegant Secessionist design cloaked in a stunning colour scheme of malachite and gold. Seating over a thousand, music sounds just beautiful here, while some clever designer managed to make the chairs acoustically positive (wooden), attractive, and comfortable (they fit the lumbar spine). I have performed there twice, and been to concerts ranging from coloratura soprano plus harp, unaccompanied Gregorian chant, baroque violins to full symphony orchestra, organ and chorus. The acoustic never fails, and the atmosphere outside is almost as good as inside. The two foyers are as beautiful as the hall, with more wonderful *art déco* tiling. Downstairs especially there is a perpetual toing and froing of Academy students, professors gossiping in corners clutching a plastic cappuccino from the *büfé* (Hungarian spelling), and lady cloakroom attendants *d'un certain âge* staring in an unfocussed manner at coffee break puzzle books while falling asleep in the midst of serried ranks of largely unoccupied coat hooks. In the middle of all this there is a rather good CD shop! The huge board for concert posters to the right of the door to the gents' loo is one of the best places in the whole of Budapest to find out about musical events, and there are more notices plastered to the various pillars that hold up the whole edifice.

Surrounding all this human activity is a truly staggering building, constructed between 1904 and 1907. Outside, a stone statue of Liszt looms over all (there is another more manic one in the middle of Liszt tér itself), and musical symbols abound in the external decoration. Inside, if – as a student, teacher or official visitor – you were to take any of the staircases up from the ground floor into the teaching areas, you would find yourself in what must still be one of the most stylish conservatoires on Earth. You would also be following in the footsteps of Mahler, Richard Strauss, Puccini Furtwängler, Heifetz, Busoni, Eugen d'Albert, Moritz Rosenthal, Casals, and many other world-famous figures, whose visits are all recorded in the famous *Vendégkönyv* (Guest Book), kept since 1894, alongside such glories as an official party from North Vietnam, one of several souvenirs of Communist times. All the luminaries of Hungarian music also passed through these portals (the side student/teacher entrance has an interior pair of swing doors that is a danger to life and limb!): Bartók, Kodály, Dohnányi, Erkel, Jenő Hubay (1858–1937, and Rector of the Music Academy from 1919 to 1934, who was once named 'the Hungarian Joachim', by someone labouring under the false impression that Joachim wasn't – well, he was),[110] and Ödön Mihalovich (1842–1929), the distinguished composer and Rector of the Academy from 1882 till 1919, of whom nobody outside Hungary has really heard. The roll call of students from more recent times is also very distinguished, and it is striking both how many achieved world-wide fame, and how many live(d) outside Hungary: Végh, Pauk, Vásáry, Frankl, Eötvös, Kurtág, Ligeti, Solti, Doráti, Fricsay, Anda, Földes, Starker, Kertész, etc., etc., etc. Such are the wages of history.

Inside, there are stained-glass panels, engraved glass panels, beautiful lettering over the doors, double doors to all the rooms, many panelled with padded leather and muttering cleaning ladies pottering about. There are three storeys of this, the corridors littered with pot plants of varying antiquity and all topped off by the mysterious *Kupola Terem* (Cupola Hall), where I recently heard one of the most remarkable musical events of my life: the rehearsal of a choir soon to make a recording of some Bartók folk song arrangements, and being conducted through the music, and on an extraordinary musico-philosophical-aesthetic journey, by one of the most amazing musicians even Hungary has managed to produce. A man I, like hundreds of Hungarians, revere, he *shall* remain anonymous.

This building is actually the third home of the Music Academy. Liszt's statue dominates the building's exterior, and his spirit still broods over the whole institution. From the outset, he was most concerned about high standards: 'The Zene Akadémia has not to work for the universally usual kind of musical study, but has indeed a weightier, higher task to fulfil ...' That the *Zeneakadémia* still retains its high international reputation today is testimony to its continuing loyalty to such exhortations.

Though nothing, I think, could take away the special place the Concert Hall of the Music Academy has in the hearts of Budapesters, recently a rival has arisen: the *MüPa*. A few years ago, the powers that be ordained that there was a need for both a new National Theatre and a new 'Palace of Arts', concert hall included. No site in central Budapest being deemed suitable, one in the rather run-down area south of Boráros tér (9th district) was eventually chosen, and the new theatre (2002) and *Művészetek Palotája* (2005), to give its full name, now stand more or less side by side grandly surveying rather a lot of empty space, which I imagine the above-mentioned powers hope will soon be a lively new arts quarter, or some such.

The National Theatre is extremely eclectic in architectural style, and I've never been inside (until my Hungarian is really very good indeed, there is probably little point). Its architecturally less peculiar companion I have visited several times, and a very remarkable place it is, inside and out. Both the walnut-lined *Festivál Szinház* (Festival Theatre), where I have heard very good chamber opera, and the 1,836-seat Béla Bartók National Concert Hall (*Bartók Béla Nemzeti Hangversenyterem*), with its huge five-manual organ and weirdly coloured walls, have again very comfortable seats, and an acoustic so fine that you positively tingle there from the physical impact of music. With several places to eat and drink, and a very good bookshop (part of the Ludwig Museum of Contemporary Art, which also lives here), it's a very pleasant place to spend several hours. The whole edifice has a wonderful feeling of spaciousness, and its outside is lit up at night by lights set into the walls themselves, a lovely 'lightening' touch. Unlike the Liszt Academy, it's hardly in the centre of town, but well worth the trip.

Away from these grand spaces, and if your taste is for chamber music, there is another unbeatable venue on offer: the Concert Hall of the Old Music Academy. Positively reeking of musical history, it is something like a miniature version of London's Wigmore Hall, and like that wonderful place, has its own very special atmosphere (and an enormous chandelier). Particularly well known are its Saturday morning recitals at 11 (organised by the Liszt Memorial Museum): one week violin and piano, the next yards of virtuoso Liszt played brilliantly by someone you've never heard of, the next a wind quintet. Tickets for concerts here are very cheap (the 600 forints you pay includes entry to the Museum itself), and only available at the door. Having left your coat with one *néni* downstairs, you buy your ticket from another on the first floor, and in you go – an old system, but again, if it isn't broken, why, etc ...? On the front door of the Old Academy, towards the end of the academic year, you can often find notice posted of diploma recitals by Academy students: well worth a try, a star could be born at any of them, or you might just get some fantastic singing or playing – and they're free.

In a capital city the size of Budapest, the musical culture of which is so lively, these halls naturally don't provide all the city has to offer in the way of musical events. Far from it – with thirty or more venues all over the city hosting regular performances of classical music, this could be a daunting prospect for the visitor. Fortunately help is at hand in the form of two very good monthly guides, both free and readily available in hotels, tourist offices, music shops, the Music Academy foyer and the like. The first and older is *Koncert Kalendárium*, which has been around for at least as long as I've been going to Budapest, and is still going strong. It uses a clever symbol guide to identify venues (the Old Music Academy is represented by a silhouette of Liszt's head, for example), and it gives full details of how and where to buy tickets. If your Hungarian really isn't up to doing this, your hotel will help, though the larger ticket agencies and all the tourist *bureaux* employ English speakers.

The other, newer guide is *Fidelio*, a rather fancier and thicker affair with lots of colour pictures, interviews with performers, critical guides, etc. It covers everything that can be included under the banner of 'culture', from opera to jazz and pop, exhibitions to dance, theatre and cinema. Like its older rival, it's in Hungarian only, and so comprehensive it can be a bit difficult to use – I recommend perseverance.

9

A composer in Budapest

All aspects of musical history and musical life in Budapest are on the large scale one might expect of a major European capital, and neither the music of the twentieth century nor the contemporary scene is an exception to this.

With composers of the stature of Kodály and Bartók casting long shadows, it is hardly surprising that lesser talents from later generations often found only a borrowed beauty with which to express themselves. To use a word of which Hungarian writers seem very fond (perhaps not realising its rarity in English usage), such epigones may succeed for a generation or so, but rarely longer. The polar opposites of Schoenbergian dodecaphony and Socialist Realism also stifled or distorted many talents. The former because, like folk song, it needs to be assimilated into a personal style in order not to become aridly mechanical, the latter because it is essentially anti-artistic.

All these influences led to a welter of music being presented to the public of Budapest (and the rest of Hungary) during the last hundred years. The names of such Budapest-trained composers as György Ligeti (who left Hungary after the 1956 Revolution) and György

Kurtág (who now lives in France) are too well known to need any commentary from me, and the subject as a whole is beyond the range of the present volume. I shall rather mention here one or two composers to whose work I have been recommended in recent years, and who are comparatively little known outside their own country.[111]

First on my list is Sándor Veress (1907–92), not even a name to me until a couple of years ago. Veress succeeded Kodály as Professor of Composition at the Music Academy, and taught the young Kurtág and the young Ligeti there before going into exile in 1949. He eventually settled in Bern, and living abroad very probably, as the person who recommended his music to me remarked: 'enabled him to achieve a wider perspective'. His work is individual, varied and of high quality, retaining its freshness after many decades.[112]

For those who, unlike Veress, stayed on under Communism, there were many artistic and political hoops to be jumped through. I was very taken with the remark made by a very well-informed source about one figure who very much succeeded in overcoming such obstacles, being presented by the Communist regime as their 'official Modernist'. Thus he became well known in the West, but for the sake of his memory he will here remain nameless: my source dismissed him as *'nem komoly'* (not serious, shallow). Quite a relief, really: a few more CDs I *didn't* need to buy.

I was very glad, however, to be able to test out another serious and positive recommendation I had received by attending *Addio*, a concert *in memoriam* to András

Szőllősy. This took place at the Hungarian Academy of Sciences on 27 February 2008, less than three months after his death. Born (like Ligeti, Kurtág – and Bartók) in Transylvania in 1921, Szőllősy came to Budapest at the age of eighteen, studying French and Hungarian at university, while taking composition lessons from Kodály. As early as 1943, he wrote a pioneering book about his teacher, *The Art of Kodály*, which is still very highly regarded. He spent the academic year of 1947–8 studying at the Accademia di Santa Cecilia in Rome with the eminent Italian composer Goffredo Petrassi (1904–2003).

On his return, he found the artistic world of Budapest in a ferment, with much music that had been ignored or unavailable during the war being performed. This heady atmosphere did not last long, however, and the grinding regime of the fifties that climaxed in the revolution of 1956 was hardly conducive to someone of Szőllősy's independent outlook finding his true artistic voice. He was also much involved in musicology, a subject he taught at the Music Academy from 1950. Thus it is only with works from the mid-1960s that Szőllősy was able to arrive at an individual style, successfully assimilating his domestic tradition and the Latin influences gained from his time in Italy.

The first such work was his *Tre pezzi per flauto e pianoforte* (1964), which also happened to open the programme of the memorial concert. This, incidentally, was free, and the *Díszterem* of the Academy packed. I had heard several people say what a warm-hearted and fine human being Szőllősy had been, and his music, too, is fine and noble,

113

full of fascinating gestures and uncompromising beauty – here, certainly, was a composer who <u>was</u> *komoly*. Unsurprisingly, there was a valedictory feel about much of the programme, and throughout the performances were of the highest quality. I shall especially never forget the pianist Gábor Csalog's mesmerising playing of *Paesaggio con morti* (1987), a work of sad loveliness, scurrying semiquavers, and bell-like chorales. This was followed by the haunting *Töredékek* ('Fragments', 1985, setting poems by István Lakatos). After the interval, there was a great intensity in the evergreen Ferenc Liszt Chamber Orchestra's rendition of Szőllősy 's *Concerto III* (1968) for sixteen strings, which has a wonderful surprise at the end, with one tubular bell striking thirteen times. On this occasion, the bell was played by Zoltán Rácz of the marvellous percussion group Amadinda, who had earlier conducted Szőllősy's striking *Addio* (2002), his last complete work, a concerto for violin and strings written in memory of the important Hungarian musicologist, György Kroó.[113] As well as an event at which almost anyone who was anyone in Budapest's contemporary music life was present, this was also a musically enthralling evening, and a salutary reminder of the importance of the physical impact of live performance in contrast to the often rather antiseptic recorded medium. The atmosphere in the hall was electrifying, with both performers and audience utterly engaged in the experience of making music.

From the side of the performing area, Szőllősy's portrait gazed out at the audience, beside it a burning candle and a book of remembrance. Before the music started, there were two speeches, one given, with his typical charm and modesty, by Zoltán Jeney. One would never have guessed his own eminence in today's modern musical scene in Budapest.

Jeney was born in Szolnok in 1943, and studied in Debrecen and Budapest, before himself spending two years in Rome as a pupil of Goffredo Petrassi. Co-founder of the New Music Studio in Budapest, his is a fascinating story that reflects the forty-year struggle of Hungarian new music under the Communist regime. Throughout the post-war period there was a lively underground of new musical activity in Budapest, in which Jeney played a prominent part. In a different political and social climate, that scene is as lively as ever, and amazingly varied. There are still neo-folklorist composers, nationalists, dodeca-phonists, minimalists, post-modernists, eclectics, all sorts, and in this Budapest is no different from London, New York, Paris, or, for all I know, Montevideo (no offence intended to Uruguayan composers: I plead ignorance). There is no need for me to encourage the open-eared visitor to embark on a sampling of these varied offerings, both live and on disc: a sort of musical wine tasting, with hopefully more swallow than spit.

Jeney himself is now universally regarded as one of the most important Hungarian composers of his generation. However, I first came across him as a performer. He is an accomplished pianist, but that was not his *modus operandi* on this occasion. Instead I can still see him on the dimly-lit stage of the *Városházi Színház* (the Town Hall Theatre in *Józsefváros*, the 8th district), seated at a little green baize table with a pile of white pebbles in front of him. For ten minutes he tapped one pebble against another, a small one against a large one (and *vice versa*): *tk, tk, tonk-tonk, tnk*.[114] Fascinating and extraordinary, and maybe just the kind of musical experience and 'happening' that worried the old-style Commies so much. What exactly was 'Capitalist' or 'decadent' about such an event beats me, let alone how it might be subversive. Mind you, I also remember Jeney telling me that when he wrote a piece in 1972, static in pitches, but dynamic in timbres, he was roundly condemned for 'importing Zen from the capitalist West': a bad case of one belief system being terrified of another, I suppose, let alone dodgy geography.

More recently, I remember vividly the premiere of his three-hour-long oratorio *Halotti Szertartás* ('Funeral Rite') in 2006: a work of amazing power and intensity. I can still see in my mind's eye, hear, and even recall the physical sensation of that performance in the Művészetek Palotája. Jeney is now Head of the Composition Faculty and of the Doctoral School at the Music Academy, and very kindly agreed to tell me about his life and career in the midst of the sort of mad schedule anyone in such a demanding role has somehow to sustain. We talked for almost three hours, so what follows is very much an edited version, without interruptions. We spoke in English – I wish that one day I might speak Jeney's mother tongue as well as he speaks mine.

I was born in Szolnok, a town in the Great Plain[115] between Budapest and Debrecen, but we lived with my mother's mother in nearby Fegyvernek, an old, old village (my father died in the war). The first person to realise that I might be musical was a neighbour, who had been Minister of Justice before the war, and despite being a fervent anti-Nazi, was sent into internal exile soon after the Communist takeover. He noticed that I was always singing (I sang Gregorian chants, imitating the priests in church), and since Grandma had an upright piano, encouraged my mother to get me piano lessons. So I began studying piano with an old lady, and made good progress. As to when I knew I would be a composer, that started suddenly when I was eleven (my first piece was a Symphony in E flat minor: lots of flats, and in the style of Beethoven). Then my mother took me to Szolnok itself to have me enrolled in a professional music school. I was still only a kid, but now I had to get up at 3.30 am to get a little local train to connect with a bigger one to go to the town and have a lesson at 7.30 am, and still be back mid-morning in time for ordinary school. Then at age 14 I went to the Music High School in Debrecen where I was lucky enough to have Zoltán Pongrácz[116] as a composition teacher – he had been one of the first composers of *musique concrète*[117] in Hungary. By that time I was already writing in a style perhaps a little like 'twelve-note' Kodály, with bits of Honegger, Schönberg and so on.

I came to the Music Academy in Budapest when I was eighteen. My teacher was Ferenc Farkas, a wonderful teacher, and he had to fight a lot for me against Ferenc Szabó, then both Rector and Head of the Composition School, who was a real Stalinist. He was notorious for having returned to the Academy after the war in his uniform as a Red Army officer, and everybody was afraid of him. Even such a senior figure as the pianist Pál Kadosa,[118] who was daring enough to include music by Schönberg and Webern in his recitals, was so intimidated by Szabó that he frowned upon a piece of mine, and told me: 'you choose a very dangerous path'. While studying composition a lot of us managed to write in an ideologically acceptable style for the exams and in a different one for ourselves. When it came to the Diploma submission we had to present two pieces. My first piece was intentionally 'acceptable', but the other, *Omaggio* for soprano and orchestra, was written in my own style, because I couldn't do it any other way. The deliberations of the Diploma panel went on and on and *on*. After four hours, Farkas came out red-faced with anger. Szabó had said of *Omaggio* that 'such music cannot exist', and there had been a huge argument. Eventually Szabó changed his tune: 'OK, he can have the Diploma *summa cum laude*. This music does not exist, but *technically* he writes it very well.'

Then I went to Italy on a scholarship to study with Petrassi at the Accademia di Santa Cecilia in Rome. I almost didn't get there. In the Ministry of Culture the people who prepared the permission

to get passports misread the information in Italian
about my scholarship, thinking it said 150,000
lire per month, when it actually was 150,000 for a
whole semester, on which I could starve, but not a
lot else. The young official who actually handed me
my passport knew better, and said: 'Get on the first
train, don't wait, or you'll never go.' I did go, but the
real state of affairs was that I hadn't got *any* money
at all, just 10,000 lire in my pocket. It was only after
arriving that I was able to apply for funding, which
I did get, and I also got fantastic teaching. The first
months were very hard because of the immense
amount of information I had to take in. At first I
just devoured all the scores and books about music
I could get hold of. I was so full of ideas, sounds
and thoughts that I got completely stuck, and told
Petrassi, 'I have *absolutely* no talent for composing'.
He was very kind, and said, 'Now you are at the
bottom, and can only go up.' Something opened
up inside me, and I could write again, and wrote
like a maniac. I won two end of year prizes – it was
a wonderful time, but there was a big problem:
the permission I got to stay in Italy was valid for
three years, but the passport for only two. So the
Hungarian authorities said: 'You must come back,
and then we'll give you another passport.' When I
went back my passport was renewed, but before I got
on the plane they withdrew it again – I never found
out why. I wanted a year at the Electronic Studio in
Milan, but it never happened.

So here I was back in Budapest in 1970, with again no money, no job, and nowhere to live. For some months I lived in a friend's garden in a log-cabin, where it was so cold that the water froze in my washbowl – it was awful. Then I got a commission for some film music, and wrote for art house films for several years. There was good money in the art films. I was even able to buy a flat. The Communists supported culture to show how well their system 'worked'. But obviously it had to be the right sort of culture, and I was already known as someone who was on that 'very dangerous path'.

Part of that path was the New Music Studio (*Új Zenei Stúdió*), which I started in 1970 with some friends. We had all been students together in the Sixties – László Sáry, László Vidovszky, Péter Eötvös and Zoltán Kocsis – and we were lucky enough to have a wonderful mentor, the conductor Albert Simon.[119] This extraordinary musician, as well as being a professor at the Music Academy, conducted a youth orchestra at the Cultural Centre (*Központi Művészegyüttes*) of the Young Communists' League (*KISZ – Kommunista Ifjúsági Szövetség*). He invited us to give a concert of our music there, which was so successful that we were asked to give another. That time half of the programme had to be cancelled at the last minute, so we substituted an improvisation on three Chinese gongs, banging them, scraping them, scratching them: all sorts of weird noises. After the concert the Head of the Cultural Centre came backstage. He was an old man, to all appearances a dyed-in-the-wool Party member. He said: 'I've been to China several times. You know, the Chinese have been doing this for 3,000 years.' But he supported us, offering us official space to practise in the Centre. So, although none of us were members of the Communist Party, we began somehow to be attached to the Young Communists' League. Otherwise we 'didn't exist' either.

For two years we just did improvisations and experiments, but when we started to give concerts in 1972, we had to put up with really harsh criticism. Communist Party cultural policy, although it was supposed to help the young and the new, was actually formulated from the three Ts: '*Támogatott, tűrt, tiltott*' (promoted, permitted, prohibited). We were never the first, but always on the line between the second and the third. I suppose it might seem odd that, being in such a position, we could enjoy strong official support, which we got from the Cultural Secretary of the League as well. To understand why you need to go back to the '56 Revolution. After that the 'Goulash Communism' of Hungary was very different from that in the other Soviet bloc countries. In '68 economic reforms had been brought in, which continued in spite of the Prague Spring and everything that happened there. In '72, though, things went into reverse, and within two years all the reforms had been stopped. Some young people in *KISZ* still believed in the reforms and were prepared to fight for them. Because we were inside the system the Cultural Secretary of the League could still stand up for us.

Official cultural policy was anyway applied in a very two-faced and hypocritical way. The government wanted to show Western Communist parties big enough (especially the Italian one, which was to be important), that an *avant-garde* music group was allowed to operate behind the Iron Curtain. We still had to put up with attacks from inside, however, especially from Tibor Sárai,[120] General Secretary of the Hungarian Musicians' Union, who led a campaign against us until 1978, when he was removed from his post by a new Minister of Culture. Even after this things were never entirely easy, but in those twenty years we must have given over 600 premieres of new music, not just Hungarian, from everywhere.

In 1979 there came a real milestone in the history of the Hungarian opposition: the famous letter signed by Hungarian intellectuals asking for the release of Václav Havel, then a political prisoner in Czechoslovakia. This was to be an open letter to the Head of the Hungarian State, the General Secretary of the Hungarian Communist Party, and the Prime Minister. The intention was to get it broadcast on Radio Free Europe. Personally I did not agree that such a letter should be broadcast from abroad, and I convinced the organisers that we should try to get the letter published openly in Hungary. So they

asked me to take it to *Népszabadság* (the official
newspaper of the Hungarian Communist Party).
I went there with Ottilia Solt (who a bit later
organised the SzETA: *Szegényeket Támogató Alap*;
the illegal Foundation for Helping the Poor, in a
country where officially there were none), and we
managed to get into the Editor's office. He went
through the roof, but then asked with a smile: 'Do
you want me to sign this as well?' Quick as a flash,
Ottilia answered: 'Well, we didn't think you'd
want to, but we would be so grateful if you did.'
Her cheek really set him off, and he started yelling
about Havel being a CIA agent, and 'what do you
Bohemians know about anything', and so forth! Then
he threatened us, saying that we hadn't better go to
any other newspapers, because he'd phone the editors
before we could get to them, and then, and then …

So the letter was only broadcast on Radio Free
Europe, but still caused a huge scandal. Everyone
who'd signed it was called in by the Personnel Officer
of his or her workplace and told to withdraw their
signature ('… I was misled …'). Since I didn't have
a real job, it was the new Cultural Secretary of the
Young Communist League who hauled me into her
office. 'You signed this? Why?' she said, shoving
the letter under my nose. I answered, 'Yes, I agreed
with what it said, so I signed.' Then she showed me
another letter that Radio Free Europe had broadcast,
in which three very daring philosophers had written
a much tougher denunciation of what was happening

to Havel. 'If you'd seen this, would you have signed it?' 'Yes, I would.' 'Well, you know, we might even *agree* with you, but what can we do – the bigger picture, you see ...?'

The Government was very crafty. They waited a few months, until international attention had shifted elsewhere, and then the reprisals started. Most of those who had put their name to the letter, my wife included, lost their jobs. Both being known abroad *and* having no job, I escaped censure, and so did the New Music Studio. Our concerts kept a flavour of protest for quite a while, though, particularly when performing pieces like Frederic Rzewski's *Coming Together*.[121]

In the 1980s slowly, slowly it got better. In '85, I got a proper job at last: from György Kroó[122] (Head of Musicology in the Music Academy), teaching his students composition. Ironically, even when the so-called Socialist state finally fell to bits in '89, there were some people who wanted the new regime to keep on running everything cultural: just change the labels and carry on as normal. At the same time the state concert management organisation also fell apart, and the new private concert organisers had no interest in contemporary music, nor any money to support it. Some people tried to start an organisation to promote new music, with both commissions and performances, but that also failed through a lack of money. The result is that Hungarian contemporary composers, except those who have lived permanently in Western countries, are actually less known abroad than they were before the change of regime.

I've always been labelled as *avant-garde*, but, you know, the concept of the *avant-garde* is changing continually. Today it's very different from what it used to be. For us it's not style that matters, just quality, and that's the same whether you're listening or composing. Cage famously quoted Stockhausen on this: 'I demand two things from a composer: invention and that he astonish me.'[123]

I had a student a few years ago who came to his first lesson extolling the virtues of Shostakovich and, like a missionary, tried to convince me of the importance of his music for the future. Although during my teenage years I'd studied a lot of Shostakovich's piano music, even performing some of it in concerts, I hadn't felt in sympathy with his music for a very long time. I didn't say a word, and though not enthusiastic enough to become a scholar of Shostakovich, I did take a look at some of his music again. This student worked assiduously, and quickly got to know lots of different composers and their different styles. By the end of the second year of his five-year course he was writing in the most extreme *avant-garde* style you can imagine. After his final exams, I said to him: 'You remember how you praised Shostakovich to the skies when we first met? I must admit I really dreaded needing to get stuck into Shostakovich for five years. But luckily for me you changed direction. How do you feel about it now?' 'Oh, I still like his music. You've never said a word directly about how I should write music, but what I learned from you is that a composer must find his own way.'

10

Eating and drinking,
seeing and buying

This is one chapter in which I am particularly glad not to be writing a guide book! Proprietors, menus, opening times, even phone numbers can change, causing endless annoyance to compilers and editors, let alone frustration to the traveller. However, musical peregrinations demand sustenance for the body as well as the spirit and the ears, so here I'll describe some coffee houses and restaurants that have come to my rescue (and much more besides), and may one day do the same for you. One additional joy to be noted is that in Budapest, when eating and drinking, your ears won't necessarily be assailed by music you didn't order. When there is background music it's more often live than not, and sometimes even good and well played ('muzak' is something of an obsession of mine: a negative one, for which I make no apologies). For readers contemplating a visit to Budapest I've also listed a couple of hotels, the addresses of some music shops and suggested purchases (CDs can also be ordered online, of course), and added a few further remarks about museums, concert halls, churches and so forth.

Just about all of the places mentioned below, except the churches, will have someone who speaks English, and menus in bars, cafés and restaurants often have an English version or at least a translation. These certainly can be as amusing as travel writers often say: how 'grey beef spit wit sun-dried plum' is supposed to get the juices flowing rather escapes me. In actual fact, Hungarian food is varied and eclectic in its origins, with many delicacies rare to the Western European palate: creamy vegetable *főzelék*, fantastic game and river fish, very filling puddings (*somlói galuska* and *mákos guba* are notorious, heaving with calories and wickedness ... and irresistible). The wines are another hidden treasure, with unusual grape types like *kadarka* and *hárslevelű*, and some wonderful names: *Cserszegi fűszeres* is quite a mouthful, already marketed as the 'unpronounceable grape' in Britain, but there are plenty of others to get the lips and tongue working before you even reach for the corkscrew.

⤚

The **coffee house** (*kávéház*) was a huge tradition in old-time Budapest, but most of the finest old places disappeared during the Communist period. Some have survived, or have been refurbished or reinvented. My favourite daytime venues have changed over the years, but nowadays I head for the **Auguszt Cukrászda** (in the courtyard of Kossuth Lajos utca 14–16) as often as I dare (they have another branch in Fény utca behind Moszkva tér, which is handy after a day tramping round the Castle District). This is still a family firm, and one that's been in business since 1870, whatever the political climate.

The cakes are fantastic, they do little open sandwiches at lunchtime, and the service is charming. Moreover, you will find yourself rubbing elbows with the cream of Budapest's bourgeoisie (occasionally still ladies wearing hats), and even tourists who know how to behave. Even better, no 'muzak', just civilised conversation.

When visiting the Music Academy, the nearby **Szamos Cukrászda** (**Royal Café**), at Erzsebet Körút 43–49 is a useful recovery point. Szamos is a famous Hungarian marzipan manufacturer, so if you like that delicious almond concoction as much as I do, this is heaven. Although it's in the same building as a newly-refurbished five-star hotel, it's by no means overpriced, and there is pleasantly tinkling live piano music on some afternoons. Near the Old Music Academy, there used to be another venue with live piano at teatime, the **Lukács** (Andrássy út 70). Sometimes the pianist sounded as though he'd put half a pint of *pálinka* in his tea, so dreamily did he play, but the place was always packed, the cakes were very good, the service warm and attentive. Now all has changed after a major revamp: the charm has gone and so have the smiling waitresses, the sleepy pianist is no more. The prices have rocketed, and the clientele has disappeared. I feared this would happen at **Művész** (Andrássy út 29, opposite the Opera House), since that was also done over recently. It was once notorious for its unsmiling waitresses, who almost snarled at the customers sometimes, so much did they love them, and also had a smoke-filled back room to be avoided at all costs. Its elegant refurbishment has cleaned the once-faded Habsburgian décor, re-upholstered the chair seats (which used to have lumps in altogether unexpected places), and overhauled the menu. Fortunately the prices haven't gone through the roof, the service has definitely improved, and so it's still busy (the big back room is now non-smoking, heaven be praised). However, I never go there in the evenings, unless the weather is warm and I can sit on the terrace (excellent for people watching). For some reason the (new?) management decided that it would be trendy to have piped music, in this case of a particularly inane variety. In the daytime it's bearable, since the volume is kept well down, but on many evenings the knob is turned up and the place becomes like any would-be fashionable bar anywhere.

Another recently refurbished place I do still go to frequently is the **Centrál Kávéház**, at Károlyi Mihály utca 9 (Pest city centre, so handy during or after a day's shopping). Usually heaving with locals and tourists in equal measure, the cakes aren't all great, but I recommend the 'multi-nut' *flódni* and the *Rákoczi torta* (jammy, nutty, gooey, yummy) – insist the milk for your coffee is *forró* (boiling), or it might be tepid (yuk!). It also usefully has a full restaurant menu, on which some things are a bit pricey, but the traditional (and typically filling) meat-stuffed pancake called *Hortobágyi palacsinta* is not, at about £3. You can also breath here (the non-smoking area is at the back on the right), and hear yourself think (live pianist upstairs in the evening in preference to thumping pop rubbish).

After seeing the many glories of the Castle District, a visit to **Ruszwurm** at Szentháromság utca 7 is essential.

This is the oldest coffee house in Budapest, a tiny place a couple of minutes' walk from the *Mátyás templom*, with wonderful cakes (try any of the *rétes*: apple, *túró* cheese, cherry, or poppy seed wrapped in flaky pastry – these are reputed to be the best in town, which I can well believe), really good coffee, and waitresses who are gratefully astounded if you speak Hungarian. This place pullulates with tourists, who do lots of pointing at the cakes and take hours to order anything. Try to get a table in the inner room, still heated by a traditional stove, (it works, so don't touch!) and take it slowly – I recommend the *borkrémroládl* ('wine cream roll', the most glorious Swiss roll in creation), a *tejeskávé* (milky coffee) or a *cappuccino*, a good book and a good hour to consume all three – this can be repeated outside in the summer. Excellent ice cream also available. **Litea**, at Hess András tér 4 (a courtyard opposite the Hilton) is also good. As its name suggests, it's a combination of bookshop and coffee shop; as to the former, it's particularly useful for the foreign visitor (not just guidebooks either), very inviting, multilingual staff, CDs and postcards on sale as well, etc., etc.; as to the latter, the cakes can be a bit so-so, but the coffee is fine – a nice place to while away the time looking at a book (or several) from the shelves, and glad to be somewhere away from the milling hordes.

﹎

Restaurants in Budapest are many and hugely varied. My first favourite was **Kispipa** (Akácfa utca 38), reputedly the first private restaurant to open in the city, even before the fall of Communism. It has an enormous menu, and not all of the dishes on the Hungarian version appear on the English one, so it's worth getting both and trying to work out what's what. The staff, well accustomed to coping with foreigners, will help you out with unflappable courtesy (how they manage this sometimes, the Lord knows, but they do!). The 'specials' are not always reliably good: I recently ate, having ordered something with quite a fancy name which I instantly forgot, one of the most boring pieces of fish ever to come my way, accompanied by taste-free spinach and stone-dead potatoes. This was the only time I've been disappointed here, and the standards, like *sólet* (a kind of bean stew), the various *főzelék* (I recommend you try a fried egg on the spinach one), and the game dishes are always really good, as are the river fish – stuffed catfish is a revelation! **Kispipa** is one of the few remaining restaurants in Budapest to serve soda water on request, rather than the more expensive mineral variety, while the house wines, which arrive in half-litre carafes, are more than drinkable, especially the *rosé*. There is a regular live pianist, who plays mainly 'songs from the shows' on a slightly clangy upright. Occasionally diners have been known to join in, especially if they've drunk a little too much: I have seen more than one slightly tipsy lady almost land in the pianist's lap.

The proprietors of **Kispipa** also own **Fészek**, at nearby Kertész utca 36: an extraordinary place, with again a vast menu, and lower prices. Some of the (older) waiters are undeniably grumpy, but the food is well worth waiting for. I really recommend this place in the summer, since a part of it is in the courtyard of an Artists' Club. You don't need to be a member to go in – just look purposeful when you enter, ignore the porter, and find your way through to the back. Sometimes there is live music in the courtyard, quite often provided by students from the Music Academy.

Another, much more elegant eatery with classy live music is **Gerlóczy** (Gerlóczy utca 1, near the central Deák tér). Elegant indeed, but not grand nor pretentious (nor expensive). Here there is a fine resident gentleman harpist from Tuesday to Saturday (evenings only), and equally fine food – don't forget to ask for bread with your meal; they make their own, and it's delicious. This place has a very nice terrace for summer eating: the square is quiet. **Articsóka**, at Zichy Jenő utca 17 (near the Opera and St Stephen's Basilica), also has a terrace, this time upstairs, and a pleasant spot it is (the piped music can be turned off on request). The service and food are good, and the prices reasonable, though the menu is rather un-Hungarian.

BORLaBOR, at Veres Pálné utca 7 (round the corner from **Central**), I have visited only once, but can thoroughly recommend. It's in a converted cellar, but is a lot nicer than that sounds, as it's spacious, and atmospherically lit and decorated. Particularly welcoming on a cold winter's evening, the food, wine (hence the name), and service were all excellent. It was packed, as **Klassz Étterem és Borozó**, on Andrássy út 41 (just north of the Opera), usually is: here you can't even book a table. If you're lucky enough to find one empty, you will enjoy a very good meal at reasonable prices (the lunchtime set menu is amazingly cheap). There is piped music, but not at a million decibels. The same is true of **Menza**, nearby at Liszt Ferenc tér 2 (even nearer to the Music Academy), although here it is a matter of putting up with the noise, which is *rather* loud, for the sake of fine eating (and drinking). Now definitely one of my favourites, this restaurant opened a few years ago as a *nosztalgiás étterem*, supposedly rekindling memories of cheap 1960s eateries, though the cooking is a great deal better! The *Sütőtökleves* (roast pumpkin soup) is a wonder, and they do top-notch roast lamb, a meat that is really hard to find in Hungary. The décor is suitably over the top, but the prices definitely aren't, and the service is first class. Across the square at number 9, **Café Vian** may be more of a bar than a restaurant, but the food is good. All the places in Liszt tér are popular with tourists and young people, so it's always lively in the evenings. For me, **Vian** is not somewhere to go in the winter, since the 'music' inside is deafening. (When it's chilly, but not *too* cold to sit outside, **Vian**, like many Hungarian restaurants, provides blankets for its customers to wrap themselves in – how civilised.)

One thing to remember in Budapest is that not everywhere yet takes credit cards. This is the one minor drawback at **Komédiás** (Nagymező utca 26), opposite the Operetta Szinház, an otherwise admirable establishment: long menu, big portions, reasonable prices, and a regular pianist, who changes from day to day, the best exponent being the Friday-to-Sunday man – he can play anything from Sondheim to Chopin with nary a wrong note, and also does requests (a 1,000-forint note helps here, slipped into the glass on top of the piano). The atmosphere is particularly pleasant downstairs, where you quite often bump into actors or singers from the nearby theatres, and there is a pleasant outside terrace. **Két Szerecsen**, at the other end of the same street (number 14, across Andrássy út) is often busy, but good value for lunch or dinner.

All the above restaurants are in Pest. The most visited part of Buda, the Castle District, is a little more 'difficult': being such a tourist-orientated area, the restaurants are often rather expensive. The **Margit Kert**, at Margit utca 15 (as described in Chapter 2), though down the hill near the river, is a godsend in any case, and closer to the Castle is the extraordinary **Szent Jupát**, at Dékán utca 3. Imagine yourself exhausted by a day's trek around the Vár, and in need of serious refuelling. Descend the hill on the little bus (or your feet if they're still functioning), totter across the concrete-ridden expanse of Moszkva Tér, over the zebra crossing and straight on past the butcher's shop. On the next corner stands this inn-like establishment, where you will be regaled with great, traditional Hungarian food and wine, friendly waiters, and enormous portions (sometimes you get pasta, rice and potatoes with a huge piece of meat *and* a sauce, all on one plate). Prices are low, it's always busy, and open into the small hours. On the hill itself, a good bar/restaurant (near **Ruszwurm**) is **Miró** (Úri utca 30), which has good cakes, salads, toasted sandwiches, and so forth. Named after the Spanish painter, it has appropriately 'surreal' furniture and fittings. There is also a small terrace in the summer, and the whole place swarms with tourists, including the rudest I've ever encountered, yelling at the waitress when *they* were in the wrong. At least they weren't Brits, but I felt really sorry for the girl, who was sadly used to such treatment. The music in the evenings here is also live, and jazzy.

The are many other places to eat on the Vár, some good, some very good, but a visit to those perhaps aimed at a grander clientele may consign your credit card to hospital. Two places at which this financial distress will be worthwhile are the **Király Étterem**, at Táncsics Mihály utca 25 (right by the Vienna Gate at Bécsi Kapu tér, the northern entry to the Vár) – the expensive joint with great gipsy music I referred to at the end of Chapter 2; and the **Alabárdos** (Országház utca 2, opposite the *Mátyás templom*, and with two high quality antique shops adjoining, one literally underneath, one next door).

Back across the river, if you're looking for grand eating, **Gundel** (Állatkerti út 2, close to the Zoo, but don't let that put you off) is legendary and fabulous. Book, dress up, order the best of everything, and enjoy. The Sunday brunch is both excellent and good value. Another place for a splendid evening is **Kárpátia** (Ferenciek tere 7–8, again near **Central**), which is delightfully old-fashioned (great décor) and has more first-class gipsy music (you may need to work out how much to give the violinist to make him go away!). **Cyrano** (Kristóf tér 7–8, just off Váci utca, phew!) is classy in an altogether different, untraditional and internationalised way, but very expensive. The last time I was there the dining chairs were covered in fluffy fabric in various pastel shades, and there was a vast sculptured thingy behind the bar; that was when it was still affordable.

If you just want to go out for a drink, Liszt tér is a good place to start (see **Café Vian** above), though in Budapest there are bars literally everywhere, usually open till late in the evening. They all serve good Hungarian beer (try Dreher or Arany Ászok) as well as beers from all over the world (especially Germany and the Czech Republic). The national drink of Hungary is wine rather than beer, and any bar will serve good national wine at reasonable prices; those serving you will usually be pretty knowledgeable and happy to help with a recommendation. Incidentally, a bar called a *borozó* might specialise in wine, and a *söröző* in beer, but don't bet on it. Many of both kinds serve meals as well.

People in Hungary, as in most civilised countries, generally go out and drink in order to enjoy themselves. Occasionally you will come across rowdy groups of drunken men: these are usually British oafs of the stag party variety, who maybe thought they were going to Prague, but can't tell the difference anyway. Hungarians who wish or need to get drunk will go to an *Italbolt* (literally a 'drink-shop'), get totally plastered on cheap beer, wine or spirits, go out into the street and fall over. The majority of people avoid these places, but they are there for those who need them. Alcoholism, especially among elderly men, is still a serious problem in Hungary, though I have never seen native drunks on the street being aggressive.

~

Hotels in Budapest are a totally different matter, being (often) not cheap at all. Catering as they do for international visitors and businessmen, prices can be surprisingly high, though not as bad as, say, London or Rome by any means. Some are very luxurious and very expensive, like the recently reopened **Gresham**; and some are huge, modern, and nice to stay in if only because you don't have to look at them from the outside (the three notorious concrete hulks on the Pest side of the Danube answer this description). A search on the internet will often reveal bargain all-in deals at centrally-sited hotels, flights included. If you want somewhere good ('three star' or thereabouts), not from a chain and not overly dear, try the **Burg Hotel** at Szentháromság tér 7 (opposite the *Mátyás templom*), which isn't fancy, but is pleasant, clean and efficient, and is especially nice if you like church bells. If you do, ask for a room overlooking the square, which shouldn't be more expensive. This is a completely non-smoking hotel with a private dental practice on the premises. In Pest, the **Hotel Peregrinus** (Szerb utca 3), just off the somewhat more civilised end of Váci utca, and near the Central Market (a fascinating place, by the way), is a little old-fashioned, but none the worse for that. The street is quiet, and some of the street-side rooms have views of the beautiful Serbian church.

~

Between your hotel and your first cake stop, you might want to buy some music (amongst other things). **Shops** are generally open from 10 am till 6 pm on weekdays, and 10 till 2 on Saturdays. Sunday opening hasn't yet hit Budapest in a big way, except in the Castle District and other touristy areas. Scores of Hungarian music, the internet notwithstanding, are still easier (and often cheaper) to buy on the spot, both new and second hand. One of the best centrally-situated music shops is **Concerto Hanglemezbolt** (Dob utca 33), a real Aladdin's Cave for the recorded music enthusiast. Though it does have new CDs, it specialises in old ones and especially in second-hand vinyl, of which it has very large stocks. Here I have seen some of the most obscure recordings to come out of Eastern Europe in the past fifty years. The staff are extremely knowledgeable, and nothing is too much trouble for them. **Kodály Zeneműbolt**, at Múzeum körút 21 (opposite the National Museum) likewise stocks new CDs, but has an amazing 'bit at the back', with some real old rarities, both in vinyl and in print. I recently found here a truly rare book published in the 1920s in Vienna, and out of print ever since: it cost me £12! The whole of this street is a gold mine for the second-hand book lover, and many of the shops have books on music, especially in German (only recently in Hungary has English finally ousted German as the second language of academe). If your interests run to the seriously historical, I can recommend the fine antiquarian music and book dealer **Vivace Zenei Antikvárium és Kiadó** at Kossuth Lajos utca 4, third floor, flat 4 (you may need to recover at the **Auguszt Cukrázda** a few doors away). Ring the bell, up you go, and see what this establishment, run by the fluently English-speaking Ádám Bősze, has to tempt you. I have seen early editions of Mozart, autograph Liszt letters, all kinds of marvellous things.[124] More conventionally, **Rózsavölgyi és Társa**, Szervita tér 5 (opposite the lovely Servite church, and near the central Deák tér station, Váci utca, the Cyrano restaurant, etc.) has probably the biggest selection of music (printed and recorded) of all kinds to be found in any Budapest shop. The staff really know what they're at, and some of them have been at it since the 1960s, with haircuts and spectacles to match. There are books upstairs, and non-classical stuff in the basement. They also sell music DVDs, concert tickets and some second-hand vinyl, and play CDs out through the shop door. The **Liszt Zeneműbolt** at Andrássy út 45 (two minutes' walk from the Music Academy) has an excellent stock of English-language books on all subjects upstairs, and lots of books, CDs and sheet music downstairs. Below ground, the lady assistants can be a bit fierce (they rarely see the light of day, after all), but they really know what they're doing, and it's also a good place to pick up your copy of *Fidelio* or *Koncert Kalendárium*.

On the recorded music front, choosing from the welter of material available, and attempting to capture the musical essence of Budapest and Hungary thereby, is hardly a simple matter, but these personal favourites of mine should be easy to find (online or on the shelf):

Gregorián ének magyarul (Gregorian Chants in Hungarian) Hungaroton HCD 32157; Schola Hungarica, cond. László Dobszay and Janka Szendrei. This group is the *non pareil* of Gregorian chant performance for me, and this disc is particularly evocative, mixing chant with medieval polyphony and *falsobordone*. If you get hooked by this one, *all* of their discs are marvellous.

Bakfark hangja (The Voice of Bakfark) HCD 32412; Voces Aequales, István Győri (lute). Voces are as good a male voice consort as you'll hear anywhere, who perform some lovely continental Renaissance motets here, while Győri plays Bakfark's complex transcriptions of them with great aplomb. Bakfark's own lute works have been recorded complete by Dániel Benkő on HCD 31564–7.

Eszterházy, Pál: Harmonia Caelestis HCD 31148–49; soloists, Capella Savaria, Pál Németh. A charming recording of this seminal work in the development of the Baroque style in Hungary. Pál Eszterházy (1635–1713), an ancestor of the Miklós of the same surname who employed Haydn, was an Imperial Prince, Palatine of Hungary, and a highly educated political thinker, poet and musician, who published this collection in 1711. How much of it he actually wrote is open to discussion, but it is charming music, sometimes näive, always melodious and delightful. Capella Savaria were pioneers in the period instrument movement here, and they and their conductor are still very much going strong.

Istvánffy, Benedek: Messa dedicata al patriarcha Santo Benedetto HCD 31782; soloists, Purcell Choir, Orfeo Orchestra, cond. György Vashegyi. Beautiful music from the second half of the eighteenth century, the work by Istvánffy unknown even in Hungary until a few years ago. (This disc also contains a recording of the *Requiem* by Joseph Martin Kraus, a fascinating figure, born in Germany, who worked for a long time at the court of Gustav III of Sweden.) Performed by a conductor, singers and players now in the vanguard of the country's historically-informed performance movement.

Erkel, Ferenc: Bánk bán HCD 11376–77; soloists, Hungarian State Opera Chorus, Budapest Philharmonic Orchestra, cond. János Ferencsik. The recording of the classic Hungarian nineteenth-century opera. This is fine music.

Liszt, Ferenc: Psalms Nos 13, 18, 23, 125, 129 HCD 11261; soloists, Budapest Chorus, Hungarian Army Male Chorus, Hungarian State Orchestra, cond. Miklós Forrai. This is such beautiful music that it's simply a scandal that none of it is better known; first-rate performances. Forrai also made a legendary recording of Liszt's great oratorio *Christus*. If you can find a second-hand copy of this, grab it and don't let go! It's only available on vinyl, and recorded semi-secretly in the *Mátyás templom* in the middle of the night in 1970. Forrai heard Weingartner conduct the work in the 1930s, and Weingartner had heard Liszt himself do the same.

Dohnányi, Ernő: Concerto for Piano and Orches-
tra No. 1 in E minor Op.5, Concerto for Piano and
Orchestra No. 2 in B minor Op.42 HCD 31555; László
Baranyay, piano, Budapest Symphony Orchestra, cond.
György Győriványi-Ráth. Wonderful works (especially
the Second Concerto) by this underrated composer.
(Nearer home, I have read strong recommendations for
the recording of the Second Concerto with Howard
Shelley as soloist on Chandos 10245; this disc also
includes Dohnányi's Harp Concertino and the Second
Violin Concerto.)

Bartók, Béla: Cantata profana; Kodály, Zoltán:
Psalmus hungaricus HCD 31503; soloists, Budapest
Chorus Hungarian Radio Choir, Hungarian Radio Chil-
dren's Choir, Hungarian Radio Symphony Orchestra,
National Philharmonic Orchestra, cond. Antal Doráti.
Excellent performances of these masterpieces (the Bartók
underperformed outside Hungary simply because of the
Hungarian text – and the fiendishly high tenor solo);
these recordings are additionally valuable for the com-
posers' own readings of the texts of each work.

Kurtág, György: The Sayings of Péter Bornemisza
Op.7, Four Songs to Poems by János Pilinszky Op.11,
Eight Piano Pieces Op.3, Eight Duets for Violin and
Cimbalom Op.4, Beads – chorus to poem by Attila
József, Splinters Op.6/c, etc. HCD 31290. Thirty-six
tracks surveying the music of this extraordinary and enig-
matic master of contemporary Hungarian music.

The Virtuosi of the Gypsy Music HCD 10212; Lajos Boross – violin, Andor Tréger – cimbalom, Lajos Boross and his Gypsy Band. Simply unbeatable playing of this repertoire.

Ájfalusi utca végig bazsarózsa (Áj Street is all Peonies) Fonó FA-078–2. It is really invidious to try to choose a representative disc from the many thousands available of Hungarian folk music, and the repertoire here isn't the most extraordinary or exotic available, by any means. However, what is particularly fascinating about it is that some of the songs were recorded in 1939, and some in 1999 – a real living tradition. There are tracks featuring a mother and then her son singing. In 1939 one old man was recorded who had been born in 1865, and in 1999 an old lady of 91. Magical.

Hungarian Folk Music HCD 18281. As it says on the front, this is 'The Legendary Folk Record'. Originally compiled as a representative disc of Hungarian folk song recording, old and new, from all over the historical territory of Hungary, it was first only presented to participants in the 17th Conference of the International Folk Music Council, held in Budapest in 1964 under the presidency of Zoltán Kodály. An earlier series of folklore discs recorded before the Second World War having long been unavailable, when this disc was later sold in shops it was eagerly seized upon, especially by those new, young enthusiasts for folk traditions soon to be important in the Táncház movement on whom it became an important influence. It was also known as the 'peacock record', from its first track *Röpülj, páva, röpülj* ('Fly, peacock, fly') used by Kodály in his 'Peacock Variations'. It was only reissued on CD in 2007.

When not browsing in music shops or sitting in live performances, there is always the radio. Radio Bartók, Magyar Rádió's classical music station is at 105.3FM when *in situ*, and also online at http://www.mr3-bartok.hu. Less afflicted by jazz and world music than BBC Radio 3, there is usually something well worthwhile listening to on this channel, in spite of the recent tendency to broadcast single movements from larger works in anthology-style programmes, especially in the mornings (classical music fans can concentrate for long periods ...). There is also quite a lot of intelligent chat, particularly after breakfast, which can be useful if you're learning the language.

⤳

Museums, as I mentioned before, are everywhere in Budapest, and about (virtually) everything. As is clear from Chapter 1, the **National Museum (Magyar Nemzeti Múzeum)**, at Múzeum körút 14–16 is an absolute 'must see', as will be the **Museum of Music History (Zenetörténeti Múzeum)** at Táncsics Mihály utca 7 (on the Vár, up the road from the Hilton), once it reopens. Also in the Castle District and this time actually in the Royal Palace, the **Budapest History Museum (Castle Museum – Budapest Történeti Múzeum)** has, besides the ancient chapel, few musically-related objects on display. The only others I came across were some exquisite Rococo painted and gilt wooden statues of musicians (including king David playing his harp) taken from the Florian Chapel in Fő utca of the Víziváros; and a beautiful presentation glass dated 1821, engraved with a portrait of Mozart, who, incidentally, never came to Budapest – he only got as far as Pozsony/ Bratislava.[125] Nonetheless, it's well worth a visit, not least because some of the temporary exhibitions have a musical theme (this is just the kind of thing guide books can't encompass). In 2001 there was one such entitled 'Sinfonia Hungarorum',[126] and another on Erkel and Liszt is planned for 2010/11. The **National Széchényi Library** is next door, but beware of attempting a visit in the summer, when the Music Collection closes altogether for about a month, to both scholars and the more casual 'group tourist'.

As described in Chapter 7, the **Liszt Ferenc Emlék-múzeum** (Ferenc Liszt Memorial Museum) at Vörösmarty utca 35 is not to be missed (tours available in English, German, French, Italian, Russian and Hungarian, but not obligatory), nor is the nearby **Kodály Emlékház** (Kodály Memorial House), at Andrássy út 89. These two are easy by public transport, but, out at Csalán út 29, the **Bartók Emlékház** (Bartók Memorial House, where the guided tour *is* obligatory), is another matter altogether. If you'd rather not do the tram/tube/bus/walk-up-the-hill-and-get-lost trek into the hillier parts of Buda, a taxi might be easier. Don't hail one on the street, they could overcharge you – from your hotel or a coffee-house (i.e. a fixed address) it will be completely 'above board'. Remember also, that

almost all museums in Budapest are closed on Mondays (the standard continental habit), and some of them open (and close) at odd times (here your standard guidebook or hotel receptionist *will* be useful!). By the way, should you be the holder of an 'International Journalists Certificate' you should get in to any of them for nothing.

Turning to places of entertainment, first stop might well be the **Magyar Állami Operaház**, at Andrássy út 22.[127] As well as the House Tour, a visit to the Shop, with its good stock of CDs, operatically-inclined gifts, and the like, is recommended. You will certainly need to consult a guide or a tourist office on the times for the tours, let alone the Shop's opening hours, which are a complete nightmare! The **Liszt Ferenc Zeneművészeti Egyetem (Music Academy)** is a few minutes' walk away at Liszt tér 8, and, with its wonderful architecture and interior décor, worth a visit even for the tone-deaf. It is soon to undergo complete renovation. Even if you don't go to a concert there, the **Magyar Tudományos Akadémia (Academy of Sciences)** on Roosevelt tér has a fine art collection and library. A tram stop or two away is the **Vigadó** at Vigadó utca 5. The original building was destroyed by a fire during the 1848 Revolution, and the rebuild in 1865 by Frigyes Feszl (1821–84), once described as 'crystallised csárdás', was in turn badly damaged during the Second World War. Since January 2004 it has been closed for renovation, with furniture piled up in the foyer. The view from outside is nonetheless striking, the façade newly cleaned. There are the inevitable memorial plaques including one to Bartók, one for the famous Liszt-Wagner concert of 1875 (see

p 21), and one put up by a Ukrainian-Hungarian Association to commemorate great Ukrainian performers such as Horowitz and Cherkassky. Many sightseeing boat trips depart from the quay on the opposite side of Vigadó tér.

Also closed at present is the **Erkel Színház** (Köztarsaság tér 30), where I had my unfortunate experience with *Lohengrin*. According to a recent interview with the National Opera House's new General Director, Lajos Vass, this house is due to reopen in 2011 as a 'multifunctional centre, with a theatre, coffee bars and conference rooms'.[128] I can only pray that it doesn't reopen with more *Konzept* on its stage. Another venue a little out from the centre of Pest is the **Művészetek Palotája (Palace of the Arts)**, at Komor Marcell utca 1, where even the tram stop has a grand name: *Milleniumi Kulturális Központ* (Millenium Cultural Centre). The tram line is nowadays a bit of a problem, being cut in half by excavations for the new Metro line 4, but if you take the simpler taxi option, beware of one thing: taxi drivers seem rather inclined to deposit their passengers round the back of the building near the public garage and the Artists' Entrances. On getting out you may well wonder where on Earth you are.

Concerning Heaven (Chapter 6), the **Szent István Bazilika** on Bajcsy-Zsilinsky út is just about the biggest thing in the road (or in Budapest for that matter), so you'll hardly miss it. The **Mátyás templom** on Szentháromság tér in the Vár seems to be permanently covered in scaffolding, but inside is even more riotously decorated than the Basilica, and its High Mass on a Sunday is almost as grand (and can last for two hours). The **Szerb templom**

also has an extraordinary interior to match its elaborate liturgical music. These and many other churches with interesting music inside and outside the liturgy I have already mentioned in the above chapter, and discussed the survival of them and their faith during the post-war period. The **Belvárosi Plébániatemplom (Inner City Parish Church)**, had to suffer the further indignity of having the Communist authorities build the Elizabeth Bridge flyover practically inside it. The church hasn't fallen down yet, despite their best efforts.[129] On a more specifically spiritual note, should you need or want to hear Mass said in English, the **Jézus Szíve templom (Sacred Heart Church)**, at Mária utca 25, run by Jesuits, has an English-language Mass every Saturday at 5 pm, though multinational in its accents.

As well as often having good concerts (lots of Bach, which is no surprise), the Reformed churches sometimes have other musical delights. Unlike the austerely beautiful **Budavári Evangélikus Gyülekezet temploma**, Táncsics Mihály utca 28 (Castle District), with its motto 'A safe stronghold our God is sure' proudly displayed over the door, the equally severe-looking **Evangélikus templom** in Deák tér, has a delightful carillon in its tympanum. Once I happened to be passing at exactly midday, and heard the *Réjouissance* from Bach's B-minor Flute Suite played at about half-speed (any quicker and I think the whole thing would have landed in the square). This was followed by Beethoven's 'Ode to Joy', just right, and a real ear-tickler: such a Germanic sound in the centre of Budapest, and nobody else took a blind bit of notice!

As for when to experience any or all of the above, it's worth remembering that Budapest has a distinctly continental climate, cold (sometimes very cold) in the winter and hot (ditto) in the summer. The wettest weather is usually in November, and the heat of August can be unbearable, especially in the flat urban expanses of Pest. The air is generally much drier than in Britain. The best times meteorologically speaking to visit the city are therefore Spring and Autumn, which fortunately coincide with the two most prestigious Budapest music events, the Spring and Autumn Festivals.[130] These are held in the second halves of March and October respectively, and have a deservedly high international reputation. April to June and September have even better weather, and there is always something interesting happening (January tends to be a bit quiet, and the Opera House season ends in mid-June, though there are performances there virtually the whole year round). I have been in Budapest in every month of the year, and have never been short of musical entertainment, whether student concert, all-star opera, folk festival, or experimental 'happening'.

Getting there: well, some brave souls drive all the way. The journey is one thing, but actually driving *in* Budapest is a real test of nerve, roughly on a level with driving in Rome. However you get there, by car, on a cheap flight, on the train via Paris, or Cologne and Vienna, go, and *Isten hozott*!

Afterword

The musical life of Budapest flows on and on, just like the Danube at the city's heart. No doubt it will always do so, though whether, as part of the world of 'classical' music, it will continue to flourish as it does today, no one can foretell. Prophets of doom would have it that the end is indeed nigh, and that the future will see us all only huddled over our computer terminals, experiencing everything second-hand through machines just like the one on which I am now typing this text. Forster's famous and horrific story of the future, *The Machine Stops*, is a particularly relevant reminder of how this might be, and what might happen if the said machine were to fail.

In the face of triumphant historicism about the music of the past and what some regard as the failure of imagination inherent in much post-modernist composition of the present day, I wonder whether the music of the future will anywhere find the synthesis that many composers say that they seek. If not, can culture survive only on the products of the past, however great they may be? The demise of the tradition of live performance and the centuries-old repertoire on which it is founded would surely be a terrible tragedy. Whether either the products of past genius will continue to retain their value, or the new music of tomorrow will be able to carry a larger proportion of the listening public with it than so often seems to be the case today must remain open to doubt (critics will always complain, but that has always formed a large part of their reason for existence, so let them).

I recently visited a temporary exhibition at the *Iparművészeti Múzeum* (Museum of Applied Arts) in Budapest, based on various private gifts and bequests. It began with the glories of medieval woodcarving, moving through the splendours of Rococo porcelain and the sensuous shapes of Art Nouveau furniture and glass before dumping us near the Exit with a larger-than-life-size black cow studded with plastic diamonds (bovine bling, and, no doubt, bling for the bovine – how very edifying!). In the light of this kind of display, and its apparently equal estimation of the beautiful and the trashy, one might well fear for the survival of any culture at all, musical or otherwise, especially with almost all education systems now being enslaved to the trendy and the politically correct, both obsessed with knowing the price of everything, and thereby understanding the value of nothing.

My thoughts on such matters, for what they are worth, remain ambiguous. No less a man than Brahms wrote, aged twenty-four: 'Who can ever say that something that never comes to an end has reached its end?'[131] Later in life he turned his back on the contemporary music of his own time, and told the young Mahler of his fears for music's future. They were walking by the side of the river Traun, a tributary of the Danube in Austria, and when Mahler responded by pointing at the river and remarking, 'There goes the last wave', Brahms replied dryly, 'Yes, but what matters is whether it goes into the sea or into the swamp.'[132]

On a more positive note György Kurtág recently said: 'One can make music out of almost nothing,'[133] and it is he who has set these remarkable words, from the poem *Bűn*[134] by the important early Hungarian Protestant writer, Péter Bornemisza (1535–84):

> *The mind is a free creature.*
> *Neither with chains nor with rope can it be*
>   *bound,*
> *but all the time, day and night, in our dreams*
>   *when we sleep,*
> *it wanders.*

A timeline

[**NB:** This is of necessity highly selective, but does contain some items not otherwise mentioned in the main body of this book; musically-related events are in **bold**.]

BC

c50,000: Prehistoric settlements existed at Érd, just south-west of modern Budapest.

c5400–4700: Neolithic period – first permanent settlements in Buda.

c2000: Bell-Beaker settlements on Csepel island (south of the city).

c1500–800: Extensive and sustained Bronze Age settlement in Budapest area includes fortifications on Gellert Hill and Castle Hill, and dwellings in Óbuda.

From early 4th century: Celtic tribes occupy Western Hungary.

During 1st century: Eravisk Celts had fortification on Gellert hill called Ak-ink[o] ('abundant water'); dense settlement of whole Budapest area.

35: First Roman invasion.

AD

106: Aquincum becomes the seat of government of Roman province of Pannonia Inferior.

228: **Water organ of Aquincum constructed.**

From late 430s: Hun domination, followed by Lombards and then Avars (from 568).

Early 9th century: Avars overcome by Charlemagne.

896: Traditional date of arrival in Hungary of Magyar tribes under the leadership of Árpád, who settles in the Csepel area of today's Budapest.

1000 (Christmas Day, or New Year's Day 1001): King St István crowned first Christian king of Hungary.

1198: **Wedding of King Imre I (1174–1204) – retinue of his wife Constance of Aragon said to include famous troubadours Gaucelm Faidit and Peire Vidal.**

1241: Tartar invasions – both Buda and Pest destroyed.

1248: King Béla IV builds the first Royal castle on Castle Hill.

1279: **Synod of Buda forbids congregations to listen to minstrels.**

1347: King Lajos I ('the Great') permanently moves the royal court from Visegrád to Buda.

1361: Buda becomes capital of Hungary.

By c1420: **'Friss' Palace of King Zsigmond completed, including surviving chapel; on several occasions during his reign the famous Minnesänger, Oswald von Wolkenstein (1377–1445) visited the court.**

1458: Mátyás Hunyadi, known as 'Matthias Corvinus', becomes King of Hungary; during his reign (until

1490) Buda becomes an important hub of the
European Renaissance.

1507: **Birth of Bálint Bakfark (1507–1576), great
lutenist and composer.**

1526 (29 August): Hungarians defeated by Ottomans at
Battle of Mohács; beginning of Turkish domination.

1541 (2 September): Sultan Suleyman makes formal
entry into Buda.

1686 (2 September): Buda and Pest are reconquered by
Christian army under Duke Charles of Lorraine.

1727: **First music school established in Buda.**

1764: **Birth of János Bihari and János Lavotta,
important composers of *verbunkos* music.**

1773: Election of the first Mayor of Pest.

1776: **First public theatre opens in Pest.**

1783: Emperor Joseph II moves the *Helytartótanács* to
Buda; first public theatre opens there.

1793: **Mozart's *Die Zauberflöte* and the first Hungarian
singspiel, *Pikkó hertzeg és Jutka Perzsi* ('Prince
Pikko and Judy the Persian') by József Chudy,
performed in Pest.**

1800 (8 March): **Haydn conducts *The Creation* in the
Royal Palace, Buda;** (7 May): **Beethoven performs
in the Várszínház.**

1810 (7 November): **Birth of Ferenc Erkel (1810–1893).**

1811 (22 October): **Birth of Ferenc Liszt (1811–1886).**

1816: **Beginning of construction of the *Vigadó*, Pest's
first concert hall.**

1838 (13–18 March): extensive flooding in Pest-Buda with 153 deaths and 829 buildings destroyed; subsequent large-scale reconstruction of Pest.

1839 (Christmas Eve): **Liszt returns to Budapest for the first time since his childhood, giving nine concerts between 27 December and 12 January 1840.**

1840 (8 August): **Ferenc Erkel's first opera, *Bathori Mária*, premiered in the newly-renamed National Theatre; Pest Singing School founded.**

1844: **Erkel's setting of Kölcsey's *Hymnus* adopted as Hungarian National Anthem.**

1848 (15 March): Hungarian War of Independence from Austria begins; Hungarian army surrenders to Russians on 13 August 1849.

1849 (21 November): Opening of *Széchényi Lánchíd* (Chain Bridge), first permanent link between Pest and Buda.

1853: **Foundation of Philharmonic Society.**

1867 (8 June): *Ausgleich/kiegyezés* (Compromise) between Austria and Hungary, forms dual monarchy, with Emperor Franz Josef crowned King of Hungary in the *Mátyás templom*; **at this ceremony Liszt's *Coronation Mass* is premiered;** huge expansion of Budapest begins; **Pest Singing School becomes *Nemzeti Zenede* (National School of Music).**

1873 (25 October): Budapest City Council holds its first meeting as the governing authority of the united city.

1875 (14 October): **First Budapest Music Academy opens at no. 4 Hal tér.**

1877 (27 July): **Birth of Ernő Dohnányi in Pozsony/ Bratislava.**

1881 (March 25): **Birth of Béla Bartók in Nagyszentmiklós, Transylvania.**

1882 (16 December): **Birth of Zoltán Kodály in Kecskemét.**

1884 (27 September): **Gala opening of Budapest Opera House.**

1887 (28 November) First electric tram service in Budapest.

1894–7: **Dohnányi studies at the Budapest Music Academy.**

1896: Millennium celebrations; (2 May) Millennium Underground railway (*Földalatti*) inaugurated by King-Emperor Franz Josef.

1899–1903: **Bartók studies at Budapest Music Academy.**

1902–6: **Kodály studies at the Budapest Music Academy; in 1906 publishes his** *Twenty Hungarian Folksongs*.

1907 (1 February): **Sándor Veress born in Kolozsvár, Transylvania;**

(12 May): **New Music Academy building opens in Liszt Ferenc tér.**

1909–10: Electric street lighting comes to Budapest.

1918 (24 May): **Premiere of Bartók's opera** *A Kékszakállú herceg vára* (**Bluebeard's Castle**) **at the Budapest Opera House;** (13 November): defeated in the First World War, the last King-Emperor of Austria-Hungary, Károly/Karl/Charles IV, abdicates.

1919: Short-lived liberal and then Communist republics rule Hungary; (16 November): Admiral Miklós Horthy arrives in Budapest at the head of his National Army.

1920 (4 June): Treaty of Trianon signed, by which Hungary's territory was reduced to almost exactly its present extent.

1921 (27 February): **András Szőllősy born in Szászváros, Transylvania.**

1923 (28 May): **György Ligeti born in Dicsőszentmárton, Transylvania;** (19 November): **Premiere of Kodály's *Psalmus Hungaricus*; Orpheum becomes Operett Színház.**

1925 (1 December): Hungarian Radio begins broadcasting.

1926 (19 February): **György Kurtág born in Lugos, Transylvania.**

1941 (1 April): Supreme Defence Council agrees to joint invasion of Yugoslavia by forces of Germany and Hungary; (June): **at the end of the 1940–1 Academic year, Ernő Dohnányi resigns as Director of the Music Academy.**

1943 (4 March): **Zoltán Jeney born in Szolnok.**

1944 (19 March): Budapest is occupied by the Germans; (11 May) **Philharmonic Society ceases to function due to the enforced retirement of all its members of Jewish origin;** (16 October): Horthy forced to abdicate; Fascist government under Szálasi installed; (27 December): Russian siege of Budapest begins.

1945 (15–18 January): Retreating Germans blow up all Danube bridges in Budapest; (13 February): Russian forces complete occupation of Budapest by seizing Castle Hill; Ferenc Szábo returns from service with the Red Army to become Director of the Music Academy, which György Kurtág joins as a student; (26 September): **Bartók dies in New York.**

1949: **Veress goes into exile in Switzerland;** (20 August): Hungary becomes a 'People's Republic'; beginning of Stalinist dictatorship of Mátyás Rákosi.

1953: **Hungarian Academy of Sciences sets up Institute of Musicology.**

1956 (23 October–4 November): Hungarian uprising against Soviet Russia crushed by Red Army invasion; (December): **Ligeti flees to Vienna.**

1957 (21 March): **Hungarian Communist Youth League** (*Magyar Kommunista Ifjúsági Szövetség*) **set up, under the auspices of which all young persons' artistic activities took place.**

1959: **Kurtág composes his acknowledged Op 1, the** *String Quartet.*

1960 (9 February): **Dohnányi dies in New York.**

1966: **Central Committee of the Hungarian Communist Party sanctions artistic works that are 'ideologically debatable and more or less in opposition to Marxism and socialist realism, as long as they [possess] humanistic value and [are] not politically hostile'.**

1967 (6 March): **Kodály dies in Budapest.**

1968: **Jeney graduates from the Music Academy.**

1970: **Foundation of New Music Studio.**

1981 (March): **First Budapest Spring Festival.**

1989 (23 October): On the 33rd anniversary of the Hungarian uprising, and to cheering crowds in a ceremony in Kossuth tér, Mátyás Szűrös, Speaker of the Hungarian Parliament declares the Hungarian Republic to be a 'free, democratic state'.

1990: Population of Budapest stands at 2,016,100.

1992 (October): **First Budapest Autumn festival.**

1993–5: **Kurtág Composer-in-Residence to the Berlin Philharmonic Orchestra.**

2000 (17 February): **Death of conductor Albert Simon.**

2004 (1 May): Accession of Hungary to full membership of the European Union.

2005 (14 March): **Opening of new National Concert Hall.**

2006 (12 June): **Death of György Ligeti in Vienna.**

2007 (6 December): **Death of András Szőllősy in Budapest.**

Suggestions for further reading

On the History of Hungary
B Cartledge: *The Will to Survive – A History of Hungary* (London: 2006); quite simply, the best in its field.

On the History of Music in Hungary
L Dobszay: *A History of Hungarian Music* (Budapest: 1993); concise and packed with information.

On Budapest
G Buzinsky: *An Illustrated History of Budapest* (Budapest: 1998); an excellent, straightforward book with very good pictures.

A Török: *Budapest, a Critical Guide* (Budapest: 2007); witty, sardonic, insightful.

Endnotes

1. The original version of this vehicle hailed from the German Democratic Republic, and in today's reunited Germany car manufacturers Herpa aim to have a prototype of an all-new version of the Trabi available in 2009 – I can't wait! It will apparently have a BMW engine. I just hope it has better springs. (See also endnote 37.)

2. Though there has been a church here since at least 1247 or thereabouts. I say 'last restored', but this is really only true in the sense that this was an almost complete rebuild, with the most extraordinarily extravagant decoration inside; these days there always seems to be scaffolding on the building somewhere.

3. B Szabolcsi: *A Concise History of Hungarian Music* (London: 1964), p 19.

4. He was not the first famous foreign musician to do this by any means. In 1198, the troubadours Peire Vidal and Gaucelm Faidit are believed to have accompanied Constance of Aragon to Hungary in 1198 on the occasion of her marriage to King Imre I.

5. Many of the free-standing churches in Budapest also have hidden gems. When attending a concert in the Inner City Parish Church (see Chapter 6), don't forget to look for the fragments of medieval frescoes, the lovely red marble tabernacles dating from 1502, and, most

extraordinary of all, a *mihrab* (prayer niche) from the time of the Turkish occupation, nestling amongst the nineteen Gothic *sedilia* behind the altar.

6. Of course, it's really only a recording, but nonetheless creepy.

7. L Dobszay: *A History of Hungarian Music* (Budapest: 1993), p 47.

8. Dobszay, p 39 quoting, J Balogh: *A művészet Mátyás király udvarában* (Budapest: 1966), vol 1, p 685.

9. See A Dobszay: *A Brief History of Music in Hungary* (Official publication of the Hungarian Ministry of Foreign Affairs, Budapest: 2001), p 2.

10. See P Király: 'Un séjour de Josquin des Près à la cour de Hongrie?', *Revue de musicologie*, vol 78, no. 1 (1992), pp 145–50, though this article is unable to quote any sources contemporary with the composer.

11. L Lockwood: 'Adrian Willaert and Cardinal Ippolito I d'Este: New Light on Willaert's Early Career in Italy, 1515–21', *Early Music History*, Vol 5, (1985), pp 85–112; A Kubinyi: 'Musikleben am Budaer Königshof, Anfang des 16. Jahrhunderts. Geschulte Musiker und Spielleute' in *Studia Musicologica Academiae Scientiarum Hungaricae*, Vol 15, Fasc. 1/4 (1973), pp 89–100; in *Adrian Willaert: a guide to research* (New York: 2005), p 383, David Kidger states that the suggestion in this latter article that Willaert may have been employed at the Buda court: 'must be treated with caution'. He was certainly in the Cardinal's retinue from October 1517 to August 1519, at a time when d'Este was re-establishing his authority over the diocese of Eger. It seems reasonable to suppose that

the Cardinal might have visited his aunt during this time
– she was instrumental in getting him his Archbishopric
of Esztergom. A contemporary chronicler Jacques de
Meyere describes Willaert as 'Cantor regis Hungariae'.

12. Now Teplička nad Váhom in Slovakia.

13. This was a rare instrument, looking rather like a cross
between a lute and a cello, on which the Prince was an
expert performer. Haydn wrote a lot of music for it.

14. Ottoman music is a huge subject, beyond the scope of
this book. To listen to some samples, access the Turkish
Ministry of Culture's own web-site at http://www.
kultur.gov.tr/EN, and follow the links to the article on
Ottoman Music and to the samples provided.

15. The reader may be more familiar with the Slavic term
'Voivode' or 'Voyevode' for these rulers, the Hungarian
equivalent of which is *vajda*.

16. K Isoz: *Buda és Pest zenei művelődése 1686–1871*, Vol 1
(Budapest: 1926), pp 10–11.

17. Named after King Matthias 'Corvinus', see pp 7–8,
its official name is the *Nagyboldogasszony templom*, or
Church of Our Lady.

18. Tommaso Albinoni, a Venetian (1671–1751); Francesco
Antonio Bonporti, from Trento (1672–1749); Antonio
Caldara (1670–1736), born in Venice, worked under
Fux in Vienna; Giacomo Antonio Perti (1661–1756), a
Bolognese; Johann Joseph Fux (1660–1741), for a long
time in the service of the Imperial court; Johann Adam
Karl Georg Reutter (1708–72), another Viennese, pupil
of Caldara, teacher of Haydn. Note that three of the four
Italians mentioned were northerners.

19. I use this designation here, since Budapest didn't officially come into existence until 22 December 1872, when Emperor Franz Josef sanctioned the regulations uniting Buda and Pest (Óbuda had already been merged with Buda in 1849); the Budapest City Council held its first meeting in the Pest Vigadó on 25 October 1873, and it is from this latter year that the union of the cities is generally dated.

20. See http://www.populstat.info (an amazing site).

21. I Keszi: *Pest-Buda* (Muzsikáló városok, Budapest: 1973), p 15; Chudy's music sadly does not survive.

22. See B Cartledge: *The Will to Survive, A History of Hungary* (London: 2006), pp 152–3 for an excellent account of the notorious Martinovics Plot, which certainly rattled a lot of gilded cages in Vienna.

23. The Palatine was an ancient office in the government of Hungary, a sort of vice-regent plus supreme judge, in earlier times appointed by the King of Hungary. From 1437 his appointment had to be approved by the Diet of the realm. In 1526, when the Habsburgs became the rulers of the areas of Hungary not under Ottoman rule, it became a life office. After 1848, it only had a symbolic role, but was not fully abolished until 1918.

24. They were both sons of the Emperor Leopold II, who had succeeded his own brother Joseph in 1790. Alexander burned to death accidentally when preparing a firework display in honour of the Empress Maria Teresa, his sister-in-law.

25. Sadly, the royal couple's marriage was short-lived: Alexandra died in child-birth on 16 March 1801.

26. Haydn's visit is commemorated by a statue sculpted by András Kocsis (1905–76) in 1959, and placed in the *Horváth-Kert* (garden) on the Western edge of the now largely demolished *Tabán*, the artists' quarter of old Buda, below the castle on the south-west side.

27. *Magyar Kurír*, 13 May 1800, as quoted in Keszi, p 16.

28. However, it was primarily a 'straight' theatre venue, and has recently become the home of the National Dance Theatre.

29. This word-order seems a little unnatural to the English speaker, but is the official translated title of this institution.

30. See K Szerző: 'The Music Collection of the National Széchényi Library', *Széchenyi National Library Bulletin* (2005), p 27ff.

31. Or, according to some sources, New Year's Day 1001.

32. Keszi, p 22.

33. In the original, five-movement version.

34. The origins of some of these figures are a little complicated (rather as in the case of Liszt): for example, Richter was born in Győr in Hungary (between Budapest and Vienna), but worked in German-speaking countries a great deal – he conducted the premiere of Wagner's *Der Ring des Nibelungen*, and was much associated with the symphonies of Anton Bruckner, as well as working at the Opera in Vienna; Joachim, of Jewish descent, was born quite near to Liszt, so his background was ethnically and linguistically German – as well as being a violinist of world renown, he was also a composer, and his works included a Violin Concerto (no

2) 'in the Hungarian Style' with a *Finale alla Zingara*. Várnay is a particularly complicated case, since she was born in Sweden of Hungarian parents. Her father retained the accent on his surname, but it would appear she never did; Mária was her mother's name. Having worked extensively in the USA, some sources refer to her as American.

35. The strictly correct term to use is 'music of the Roma', which is of course a huge subject far beyond the scope of this book, not least since it also extends far beyond the boundaries of Hungary, past or present. I use the phrase 'gipsy music' because of its greater familiarity to a non-specialised audience, and I intend no slight to this wonderful music, to its performers, nor to the Roma themselves. The music the Budapest gipsies play is in any case very different from the indigenous folk music of the Roma peoples.

36. Ungarescas and the like can be found in Wolf Heckel's *Lautten-Buch* (1556) and Jacob Paix's *Ein schön, nutz und gebreuchlich Orgel Tabulaturbuch* (1583), as well as in contemporary collections of French and Italian origin.

37. A Hungarian–German Pocket Dictionary (*Magyar és német zsebszótár*), published in Buda in 1838, gives 'Trabant' as one German equivalent of *hajdú*. This *can* mean 'gentleman-at-arms' in English, though I rather think the more colloquial alternative 'hanger-on' is a great deal more appropriate for the ubiquitous 'Trabi' car of Communist times in Hungary, which often did feel as though it, let alone its passengers, *were* hanging on – just! The meaning originally intended for the car was

'fellow traveller' or 'satellite', and the name was inspired by the Soviet Sputnik.

38. Cartledge, pp 105–6; haiduks later settled in Eastern areas of 'Royal Hungary', and to this day there is a county called 'Hajdú- Bihar', centred on Debrecen, in which there are a number of cities, towns and villages with 'hajdú' as the first part of their name. The figure of a haiduk brandishing a weapon features prominently in the coats-of-arms of several of these places, and people in this part of Hungary are very proud of their particular heritage. 'Hajduk Split' is a high-ranking Croatian football team.

39. From Encyclopaedia Humana Hungarica 05: Balázs Sudar, *Cross and Crescent: The Turkish Age in Hungary (1526–1699)*; online at http://mek.niif.hu/01900/01911/html/index14.html

40. Dobszay, p 96.

41. Szabolcsi, p 54.

42. Szabolcsi, p 54.

43. Szabolcsi, p 56.

44. Szabolcsi, p 56.

45. Szabolcsi, p 57.

46. From the journal *Honderü*, first published on 7 January 1843, of which Petrichevich was first editor and then, from 1845, proprietor.

47. Sándor Petőfi (1823–49) was an important nationalist Hungarian poet, a key figure in the 1848–9 War of Independence, and remains a great hero for Hungarians. This quotation is my translation from Petrichevich's entry in the *Magyar Életrajzi Lexikon* (Hungarian

Dictionary of National Biography, available online at: http://www.mek.iif.hu/porta/szint/egyeb/lexikon/eletrajz/html/index.html

48. Quoted on p 264 of J Frigyesi: 'Bela Bartok and the Concept of Nation and "Volk" in Modern Hungary', *Musical Quarterly*, Vol 78, no 2 (Summer 1994), pp 255–87. The remarks were made to another folklore researcher of the period, the writer Dezső Malonyay (1866–1916), who was working in the Székler region. The Székler (*Székely*) are an ethnically Hungarian group living mainly in the Eastern part of Erdély, now Romanian Transylvania. In Budapest I have heard the word 'peasant' used as a term of rebuke very recently.

49. In Frigyesi, see note 48.

50. Szabolcsi, pp 84–91.

51. 'Folk costume' is here, and not surprisingly, a ludicrously over-general term: in former times every region of Hungary, and in some cases every village, had many different types of costume for different occasions, social classes, sexes, ages and so forth. Of course, in this it differed from no other country. I strongly recommend a visit to the *Néprajzi* (Ethnological) *Múzeum* opposite the Parliament building, a wonderful, utterly unboring place.

52. Part of a process seen in every country as it becomes more industrial and more urban, which mainly happened in Hungary much later than in, for example, Britain.

53. The halls where the Táncház movement held its meetings were also, and importantly for the Communist regime,

social meeting-places that had nothing at all to do with that much older power base, the Church.

54. And thence to Youtube.

55. Bartók ruefully recounts such adventures in a long letter to Stefi Geyer dated 16 August 1907 (see *Béla Bartók Letters*, ed J Demény, pp 70–4 [English trs. London: 1971]). There are also important links between folk song and liturgical chant, which I have no room to discuss here.

56. The last word means 'town centre', though this is really now only another district of Budapest, and not *that* far from the centre: compared to London or New York, nothing is.

57. Ed F Sebő: *A táncház sajtója* (Budapest: 2007), pp 78–9.

58. Open M–T 2 pm – 5 pm, W–F 2 pm – 10 pm, S 7 pm – 11 pm, closed Sundays.

59. At http://db.zti.hu/br/index_en.asp

60. His folk music collection, the *Kodály Rend*, is regarded as every bit as important as the Bartók collection mentioned earlier.

61. Taken directly from the English pages of their web-site: http://www.heritagehouse.hu/index.php?page=796

62. László Lajtha (1892–1963) worked with Bartók and Kodály on their folk music research, and later became Director of Music for Hungarian Radio and Director of the Museum of Ethnography. He also had a fine reputation as a composer, especially of symphonies, though this reputation suffered under the Communists as a result of his support for the 1956 Hungarian

Revolution, and has only recovered comparatively
recently.

63. Though this book is supposed to be about music, all
aspects of folk culture are so deeply intertwined that
strict compartmentalisation seems hardly appropriate.

64. I note that Hungarian folk musicians, playing on the
phrase for serious music, *komoly zene*, sometimes refer to
its practitioners as those who play or study *szomorú zene*
(sad music).

65. I wondered whether such different-looking instruments
could have the same name, but was assured this was so by
the players themselves. I hope I have not misrepresented
what they told me!

66. The standard of work displayed is also of a much higher
standard than that usually encountered at craft fairs
in Britain, and ranges from hand-woven textiles in
traditional patterns to pottery, glass, woodware, wrought
iron, jewellery, etc. There are also a couple of very good
stands selling books and music with folkloric links and
the food stands are simply wonderful. The fair runs from
early December until New Year's Eve. Sometimes there is
another one there before Easter, and something similar
usually takes place during the summer in the precincts of
the Royal Palace in the Castle district.

67. http://www.folkradio.hu.

68. Transcribed by me from a wall in a room in a temporary
exhibition in 2007 at the Ethnological Museum entitled
Síppal, dobbal, didszeriduval ('With pipe, drum and
didgeridoo'), that belied its, to me, rather odd title by
being absolutely fascinating. (I later realised that it was

a play on the title of a work by György Ligeti: *Síppal, dobbal, nádihegedűvel* – 'With pipes, drums, fiddles', itself a quotation from the old Hungarian children's song, *Gólya, gólya, gilice*.) Amongst a world-spanning display of folk instruments, other exhibits of particular interest included lovely photographs of Bartók on his 1936 folk song collecting expedition to Turkey, extraordinarily evocative recordings from the same journey, and some of the very wax cylinders he used.

69. In 'Magyar népzene és új magyar zene', ('Hungarian Folk music and New Hungarian Music', *Zenei Szemle*, Vol 12, nos 3/4, pp 55–8 (Budapest: 1928).

70. In 'Gyermekkarrok' ('Children's choirs', *Zenei Szemle*, Vol 13, no 2, pp 1–9 (Budapest: 1929); my translation.

71. Quoted by Bartók in his article 'A népzene jelentőségéről' ('On the significance of folk music'), *Új idők* 37/26, Budapest (June 1931), pp 818–19.

72. He was also a chess player of international standing – quite a Protean figure.

73. This was an enlarged version of the original, a short, fifteen-minute stage work, first performed in 1924.

74. The roll call of those involved in the opera house's building and/or decoration reads like a 'Who's Who' of artistic Budapest at the time.

75. I make no apologies for the preponderance of Wagner on this list – it's much easier to afford his operas in Budapest than in London!

76. The 2008 opera production at this festival was Verdi's *Otello*, featuring Mr F as Iago, and very good he was. A

fellow Russian singing the title role did all the shouting instead.

77. To translate partially the title of A Batta: ... *álom, álom, édes álom* ... (Budapest: 1992), an excellent book on the Budapest operetta. This title is a quotation from the Duet of the Bon Vivant Prima Donnas in Kálmán's *Csárdáskirálynő*, and the phrase became a motto for the whole genre of Hungarian operetta.

78. Try www.ticketportal.hu, and press the Union Jack symbol in the top right-hand corner.

79. My translation of a quote from an interview given by Kálmán to a Vienna newspaper in 1913; see Batta, p 7.

80. Sadly this all-male group is now finding it so difficult to recruit boy singers that it has perforce become an ATB ensemble.

81. Incidentally, this is also a city where, in order that people may visit one another on Christmas Day, public transport works, so that no Budapester need be forcibly marooned in the prolonged and peculiarly British agony known as a 'family Christmas': British transport authorities please note! Hungary is a country of many public holidays, on all of which public transport functions very well.

82. Mind you, English singers still generally pronounce the Latin of Bach, Haydn and other German-speaking composers in an Italian manner, or even worse, perpetrating such delights as 'in egg-shell-sees', whatever that's supposed to be!

83. Reporting the acting of the great castrato Nicolini in *The Tatler* for 3 January 1710.

84. In that year King Géza of Hungary negotiated a treaty with King Henry II of Bavaria, fixing this boundary, which remained until the Treaty of Trianon in 1920.

85. R Taylor: *Franz Liszt* (London: 1986), pp 2–3, who here disagrees with the notion, as expounded in, for example C Lubliner, *How Hungarian was Liszt?* (available online at http://www.ce.berkeley.edu/~coby/essays/liszt.htm) that the spelling was adopted by Liszt's father Ádám, to make the name easier for Hungarians to pronounce.

86. Quoted by Lubliner, see note 84.

87. This work was never performed during Liszt's lifetime. The first performance was on Good Friday 1929 in the Belvárosi Plébániatemplom. The version with organ was Liszt's original, not published until 1936. He also made a version not for church use, with the accompaniment arranged for piano duet (see the recording on HCD 31424).

88. As discussed in, for example, P Merrick: '*Le chasseur maudit*. Key and Content in Liszt's Music in C Minor', *Studia Musicologica Academiae Scientiarum Hungaricae*, Vol 44/3–4 (July 2003), pp 321–35.

89. As quoted in H Searle: *The Music of Liszt* (New York: 1966), pp 5–6.

90. A fascinating general study of Liszt's work is P Merrick: *Revolution and Religion in the Music of Liszt* (New York and Cambridge: 1987, reprinted 2008), not as well-known a book as it should be.

91. Now the Belvárosi Plébániatemplom, see p 110.

92. In 1856 Liszt requested to become a third order member of the Franciscan order at Pest, but only became such at a formal presentation there in 1858.

93. In Hungary, flats are always designated by the number of rooms they contain, plus kitchen and bathroom, so a 'three-room flat' really has five, and would have been quite spacious.

94. Letter of 28 July 1877, to the first Secretary of the Academy, Kornél von Ábrányi; see http://www.fullbooks.com/Letters-of-Franz-Liszt-Volume-2--From-Rome6.html, in which it is letter no 212.

95. This is one of the three notoriously hideous lumps of hotels disfiguring the Pest bank of the Danube. Modern hotels don't have to be ugly: like many people I have serious doubts about the Hilton up on the Vár, but Le Méridien on Deák tér was very well done.

96. From the Introduction to his book *Hungarian Folk Music* (London: 1931).

97. M Gillies (ed): *Bartók Companion* (London: 1993), p 110.

98. The accent on every Hungarian word is on the first syllable. The absence of any upbeat necessarily makes for a very distinctive style of word setting, and, when published with alternative words in other languages, a lot of changes to rhythms and sometimes even notes need to be made.

99. This was not because of any fears due to the First World War: Bartók had been rejected for military service. The existence of this letter is reported by Bartók's son, Béla junior, in M Gillies (ed): *A Bartók Companion* (London:

1993, p 23), but is in neither the original Hungarian edition of Bartók's letters, ed. J Demény (Budapest: 1976), nor in the English translation (London: 1971).

100. J Ujfalussy, tr R Pataki: *Béla Bartók* (Budapest: 1971), p 116.

101. In a postcard to Etelka Freund dated 24 November 1911; see Ujfalussy, p 117.

102. *Az Újság*, 25 December 1912, quoted in Frigyesi, op. cit., p 276. What a charming Christmas present!

103. Referring to, amongst other works, the book *Racial Problems in Hungary* (London: 1908), written under the pseudonym 'Scotus Viator' (Scottish Traveller) by the British historian R W Seton-Watson.

104. Quoted in Ujfalussy, pp 119–20; see also J Kárpáti, 'Bartók Béla kereszttűzben' ('Béla Bartók in the Crossfire'), in *Forrás*, vol 38/no 3 (March 2006), pp 22–43.

105. Letter to Géza Vilmos Zágon, dated 22 August 1913; see *Letters*, ed Demény (London: 1971), pp 123–4.

106. A short-lived Communist regime was ousted by the right-wing regency of Admiral Horthy in 1920.

107. Now Rákoskeresztúr, in the 17th district of Budapest.

108. Letter to Jenő Zádor, dated 1 July 1945; see *Letters*, p 347.

109. Another take of this statue now stands outside London's South Kensington tube station, marking Bartók's friendship with the English composer Peter Warlock (1894–1930).

110. See endnote 34 for more details about Joachim.

111. For anyone interested in this fascinating subject, I heartily recommend R Beckles Willson: *Ligeti, Kurtág*

and Hungarian Music during the Cold War (Cambridge: 2007).

112. Try Hungaroton HCD 32010, 32013 and 32118 for a representative sampling of his music.

113. Several of these works can be found on HCD 31727, which also includes probably his best-known work outside Hungary: *Fabula Phaedri*, written for the King's Singers in 1982.

114. A piece by Christian Wolff (b 1934), an American experimental composer associated with Frederic Rzewski (see note 120) and the English *avant-gardiste* Cornelius Cardew (1936–81).

115. This is the large flat area of eastern Hungary, known as the *Alföld*.

116. Zoltán Pongrácz (1912–2007), Professor of Composition at Debrecen (1947–58) and of Electronic Composition at the Budapest Music Academy (1975–95).

117. An early form of electronic music using pre-recorded materials of all kinds; introduced in about 1948 by the French composer Pierre Schaeffer (1910–95).

118. Pál Kadosa, pianist and composer (1903–83), later the teacher of Zoltán Kocsis, Dezső Ránki and András Schiff.

119. Universally renowned in Hungary as a conductor, Simon (born Makó 18 August 1926) is little known outside, and disgracefully under-represented on disc. A fine sample of his art is his recording of Schubert's Symphony No 9 in C, made in 1979 with the orchestra of the Liszt Ferenc Academy of Music (BMC CD 109).

120. Tibor Sárai (1919–95) learnt Composition privately with Kadosa; he was Head of Music at Hungarian Radio (1950–3) and a teacher at the Bartók Specialist Music High School in Budapest from 1959, when he also became General Secretary of the Musicians' Union.

121. Frederic Rzewski (b 1938); American composer. Frequently inspired by social and historical themes and events, his music often features improvisational elements. *Coming Together* sets letters by Sam Melville, an inmate of the State Prison in Attica, New York State, scene of famous riots in 1971.

122. György Kroó (1926–97), an important Hungarian musicologist and critic, wrote major works on Schumann, Berlioz, Wagner and Bartók, amongst others.

123. From *Indeterminacy: new aspects of form in instrumental and electronic music. Ninety stories written and read by John Cage, with music by David Tudor and John Cage.* Smithsonian/Folkways CD SF 40804/5, 1992 (this quotation at between 13' and 14' approximately).

124. Also online at http://www.vivace.hu

125. There is a long-standing legend that Mozart also visited Győr. This is not true.

126. After the famous story from the time of King St Stephen. One master Walter, who, asked by his bishop what was the song being sung by a maid-servant as she turned a stone handmill, gave it this title; see Dobszay *A History of Hungarian Music*, Corvina, 1993, p 19.

127. If you're feeling grand and want to dress up, or even better, carriage-and-four are equally ac wonder if the latter is still true; it's very tem

179

128. See the October 2007 issue of the tourist magazine *Servus*, online at http://www.servus.hu/interju/okt_2007.php

129. Of course, there was an Elizabeth bridge before the Second World War, but the old one ended considerably further from the church.

130. See http://www.festivalcity.hu and http://bof.hu for further information.

131. In a letter to Clara Schumann dated 11 October 1857, quoted in H A Neunzig: *Johannes Brahms* (London: 2003), p 120.

132. Neunzig, p 121.

133. R Beckles Willson: 'The Mind is a Free Creature: The music of György Kurtág', *Central Europe Review*, Vol 2, No 12 (27 March 2000).

134. As the second of his Op 7, *The Sayings of Péter Bornemisza* (1968).